RAILWAYS

RAILWAYS

HOWARD LOXTON

HAMLYN
LONDON·NEW YORK·SYDNEY·TORONTO

CONTENTS

Published by
THE HAMLYN PUBLISHING GROUP LIMITED
LONDON · NEW YORK · SYDNEY · TORONTO
Hamlyn House, Feltham, Middlesex, England
© The Hamlyn Publishing Group Ltd 1963
Revised edition 1970
Reprinted 1972
ISBN 0 600 03332 5
Printed in Holland by Senefelder, Purmerend

ABOUT THIS BOOK

THE CHANGES which railways brought to the economic and social life of the world were so far-reaching that the first railways seem to have belonged to a time remote from our own, yet, only 150 years ago, no public railway existed. Those early railways were a symbol of modernity to contemporary people and epitomised the aggressively advancing spirit of their age. Today, although earthworks, tunnels, viaducts and stations built by the pioneers are still in use, the railways themselves are going through a great period of change: new forms of power and automation are transforming their appearance and operation.

Railways combine past and present, and with every train that passes they link our thoughts with places far away. The locomotive itself is a personification of speed and power. As a small boy I remember being taken, for the first time, to meet the driver at the end of a railway journey, and I was so frightened of the monster of steel and steam that I would not go on to the footplate.

The railways have romance, but they have too a fascination for the technically and mechanically minded, with their complex organisation and operation and the excitement of new developments in locomotives, permanent way and signalling.

This book reflects all these facets of the railway's character. It adds to the historic record of the first railways and the stimulating picture of the railways' future, the comments in words and pictures of writers and artists both of those early days and our own times. However, it is not the writers, artists and historians who have made the railways what they are, but the engineers and architects, the railwaymen — drivers, firemen, signalmen, cleaners, station masters, ticket clerks — everyone who helps in running them. It is their achievement that this book records.

THE SONG OF THE IRON ROAD

Engine driving's got to be in your blood for a start. If it's not in your blood to stand the erratic hours you'll never stand the pace. The railway life, to my mind—to the proper railwayman—it always comes first, it's in his blood. (ALEC WATTS — Chargeman Cleaner)

The old railwayman, it was a tradition, it was part of your life—railways went through the back of your spine like Blackpool went through rock. (JIM HOWARTH—Driver)

What a feeling you have when you get off the shed; you've got the engine, you've got the control of it, and what a feeling—'I'm cock of the bank, there's nobody can take a rise out of me now, she's mine.' Come on, me old beauty, and off we go. The moon's out and the countryside—it's lovely. On we go, what a feeling—she answers to every touch. 'Some more rock on, lad.' Yes—it's grand. (JACK PICKFORD—Driver)

The iron road is a hard road and the work is never-ending,
Working night and day on the iron way
We're the boys who keep the engines rolling.

You sign on at the loco-shed, they put you on the cleaning . . .
In your dungarees cleaning super Dees . . . . you're a
Sweeper-upper, brewer-upper, shovel-slinger, spanner-bringer,
Steam-raiser, fire-dropper, general cook and bottle-washer,
Learning how to keep 'em rolling.

'Here, lad, fetch me a bucket of red oil for a red tail lamp!'
Charlie!
'Charlie!'
On your toes!
Clean that muck out of number five.
'Look alive there.'
Get weaving!
'Where you going for that oil? Arabia?'
See the job on number three,
They're gonna strip her.
'Hey, Ginger!'
Leave the job you're working on,
Help the Fitter.
Hold the light,
The one inch spanner off the bench,
The one inch reamer!

y, cleaner!'

this! Do that!
me this! Get me that!
ush job on number eight
rking late, got a date,
ever make it.

'll have to break it!
ST A BLOODY SKIVVY THAT'S ME!'
o years,
e years,
a years,
teen years a cleaner.

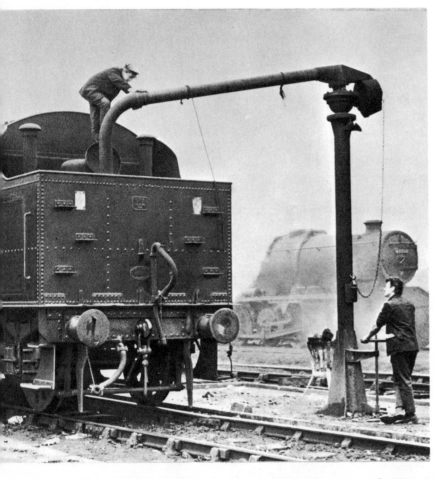

hen you've done your time at the loco shed
d had your share of trouble,
the old footplate you're the driver's mate,
d you're married to a lousy shovel.

check the water, check the tools,
d chuck the blooming coal in;
ve the gauge a wipe, check injector-pipe,
ow it's:

Swing your shovel at the double,
Give her rock, watch the clock,
Steam raising, sweat running,
Back aching, bone shaking,
Fireman, fireman, keep her rolling.

When you've shovelled a million tons of coal
Some ten or twelve years later;
And your only dream is of raising steam,
Then they hand to you your driver's papers.

7

You're on your own mate,
King of the footplate.
You've got a load mate,
Watch the road mate.
Get her through mate,
It's up to you mate.

She's a class eight engine
She's as tough as they come.
Weighs well over a hundred tons.

She's a puller,
An iron horse.
You've got nine tons of coal
You've got four thousand gallons of water.

You've got her measure,
Her boiler pressure is
Two hundred and twenty-five pounds an inch.

You've got a snorter.

You've got to watch the line
And get her there on time
And keep her rolling.

Keep your hand on the brake
She's a monster mate,
That you're controlling.

The iron road is a hard road and the work is never-ending
Working night and day on the iron way we're the

Loco-drivers, early risers, lodging turners, mile burners,
Eleven-quid-a-week earners,
We're the boys who keep'em rolling.

(FROM THE BALLAD OF JOHN AXON
by Ewan MacColl, Peggy Seeger and Charles Parker)

THE BEGINNING OF RAILWAYS

NO ONE KNOWS who first invented railways, but we do know that the ancient civilisations realised that wheels moved more easily over a smooth surface, and that the Greeks, Romans and Assyrians used grooves cut in stone slabs as guide tracks for their vehicles, for the grooves have outlasted their makers by two thousand years.

Heavy carts with wooden wheels soon wore ruts into the soft roads of Elizabethan times. Someone discovered that if boards were put into the ruts before they became too deep horses could haul their carts much more easily. Lines of wooden rails came into use in Britain's mines some time after 1600. Roger Worth described tramroads at Newcastle in 1680: 'The manner of the carriage is by laying rails

wheels to give greater strength they soon wore out the wooden rails, which then had to have iron plates fixed to them. As early as 1738 there is a report of cast iron rails being substituted for wooden ones, but the wagons were too heavy for them. The use of smaller wagons linked together dispersed the weight and solved this problem. In 1765, however, wooden rails were still being laid: 'When the road has been traced at six feet in breadth, and where the declivities are fixed, an excavation is made of the breadth of the said road, more or less deep according as the levelling of the road requires. There are afterwards arranged along the whole breadth of this excavation, pieces of oak wood of the thickness of four, five, six, and even eight inches square: these are placed

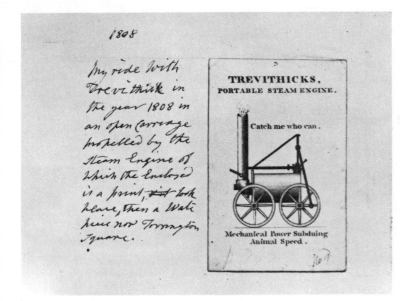

1

2

of timber from the colliery down to the river, exactly straight and parallel, and bulky carts are made with four rowlets fitting these rails, whereby the carriage is so easy, that one horse will draw down four or five chaldron of coals, and is an immense benefit to the coal merchants.'

When iron tyres were added to the wooden

1 Richard Trevithick's *Catch Me Who Can,* a print kept as a souvenir by one of the passengers on the experimental railway.
2 A portrait of the inventor painted by Linnell in 1816 when Trevithick was forty-five.

across and at the distance of two or three feet from each other: these pieces need only be squared at their extremities, and upon these are fixed other pieces of wood, well squared and sawed, of about six or seven inches breadth by five in depth, with pegs of wood; these pieces are placed on each side of the road along its whole length; they are commonly placed at four feet distance from each other, which forms the interior breadth of the road.'

With the harnessing of steam power in the mines, iron became cheaper and cast iron rails became more usual. These railways operated by man-power, horse-power, or sometimes by a rope attached to a stationary engine. In 1759

1

2

1 A drawing by Thomas Rowlandson showing the circular railway at Euston Square in 1809.
2 A tram wagon from the horse-drawn railway from Stratford to Moreton-in-the Marsh dating from 1826, the year the line was opened. It stands on a section of the original line which was fastened to square blocks, not wooden sleepers.
3 A poster giving charges on the Surrey Iron Railway.
4 William Hedley's locomotive *Puffing Billy* of 1813.

James Watt, who had developed the steam engine, is believed to have experimented with steam power in a locomotive, and his assistant William Murdock made a working model which is still preserved in the Birmingham Museum of Science and Industry. In France, Joseph Cugnot built a steam engine for operation on the highway in 1769, but the first locomotive to run on rails was built by an Englishman, Richard Trevithick. Trevithick developed his own road vehicle (which when first tried out in 1801 broke down after 300 yards and later set fire to the coach-house of the hotel where Trevithick was recovering) and then built a locomotive which he demonstrated in 1804 on Pen-y-Darran Ironworks Railway in Wales. It carried ten tons of iron ore and seventy passengers in five wagons, at five miles per hour along a ten mile line. Four years later Trevithick tried to rouse public interest by building a circular track on some waste land near where Euston Station stands today. For a shilling Londoners could travel in open carriages pulled by a locomotive called *Catch Me Who Can*.

All the early railways were operated for private use, but three years before Richard Trevithick's success at Pen-y-Darran the World's first public railway was chartered by an Act of Parliament — on 26th July 1803 it was opened between Wandsworth Wharf and Croydon. Although flanged wheels had been known in Germany since the mid-sixteenth century and were used in Great Britain at Bath as early as 1731, these cars had smooth wheels and ran on angled rails.

Others followed Trevithick's lead; one man, called Brunton, tried to make a locomotive which walked like a horse! William Hedley, at one time Trevithick's agent and a director of Wylam Colliery, Durham, designed a locomotive very like the *Catch Me Who Can* and took out a patent in 1813 with Mr. Blackett, owner of the colliery. They called the locomotive *Puffing Billy*.

George Stephenson, an engineer from Wylam, at this time working at a Killingworth colliery, saw Trevithick and Hedley's machines and with the encouragement of Lord Ravensworth built a locomotive which, on 25th July 1814, drew eight carriages weighing twenty tons up a slight ascent. In 1815, he took out a patent for his locomotive, which he named the *Blücher*.

Stephenson became technical manager of the Stockton and Darlington Railway in 1823. The company was formed in 1821 and the line was opened publicly on 27th September, 1825, with a train drawn by 'Locomotive No. 1.'

3

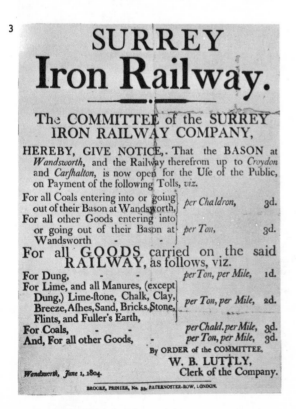

4

THE OPENING OF THE STOCKTON AND DARLINGTON RAILWAY

THE 'NEWCASTLE COURANT,' 1st OCTOBER 1825

ON TUESDAY LAST, September 27th, 1825, that great work, the Stockton and Darlington Rail-Way, was formally opened by the proprietors, for the use of the public. It is a single Rail-Way of 25 miles in length, and will open the London market to collieries in the western part of the county of Durham, as well as facilitate the obtaining of fuel to the country along its line and the northern parts of Yorkshire.

The line of Rail-Way extends from the collieries in a direction nearly from west to east, from Witton Park and Etherly, near West Auckland, to Stockton upon Tees, with branches to Darlington, Yarm, etc., and is chiefly composed of Malleable Iron Rails. At the western extremity of the line, a deep ravine occurs at the river Gaunless; on the summit of the hills on each side of which permanent steam-engines are fixed for the purpose of conveying the goods across the two ridges. The engine on the western side of the vale is called the Etherly Engine, and that on the eastern side the Brusselton Engine; the latter of which, in addition to conveying the goods up from West Auckland, also continues the transit down the eastern side of the ridge: below this, to the east, the country, though undulating, is pretty flat, and the conveyance is performed by locomotive engines. To give eclat to the public opening of the road, a programme was issued, stating that the proprietors would assemble at the permanent

Brusselton Inclined Plane.

Train of Waggons crossing the Turnpike Road near Darlington.

Train of Waggons drawn by a Locomotive Engine.

2

1 Dobbin's contemporary sketch of the opening of the Stockton and Darlington Railway in 1825.
2 Scenes on the railway: the Brusselton tower and inclined plane; a train of wagons crossing the turnpike road near Darlington (note the mounted rider leading the procession); a train of wagons drawn by a locomotive.
3 The world's first railway ticket office: this cottage was used as a booking office for the Stockton and Darlington Railway.
4 Locomotive No. 1: *Locomotion.*

steam-engine below Brusselton Tower, about nine miles west of Darlington, at eight o'clock. Accordingly, the committee, after inspecting the Etherly Engine Plane, assembled at the bottom of Brusselton Engine Plane, near West Auckland, and here the carriages, loaded with coal and merchandise, were drawn up the eastern ridge by the Brusselton Engine, a distance of 1960 yards, in seven and a half minutes, and then lowered down the plane on the east side of the hill 880 yards in five minutes. At the foot of the plane the locomotive engine was ready to receive the carriages; and here the novelty of the scene and the fineness of the day had attracted an immense concourse of spectators—the fields on each side of the Rail-Way being literally covered with ladies and gentlemen on horseback, and pedestrians of all kinds. The train of carriages was then attached to a locomotive engine, of the most improved construction, and built by Mr. George Stephenson, in the following order:

1. Locomotive engine, with the Engineer, (Mr. Stephenson,) and assistants. 2. Tender, with coals and water; next, six waggons loaded

3

4

with coals and flour; then an elegant covered coach, with the committee and other proprietors of the Rail-Way; then 21 waggons, fitted up on the occasion for passengers; and last of all, six waggons loaded with coals, making altogether a train of 38 carriages, exclusive of the engine and tender.

Tickets were distributed to the number of near 300, for those whom it was intended should occupy the coach and waggons; but such was the pressure and crowd, that both loaded and empty carriages were instantly filled with passengers. The signal being given, the engine started off with this immense train of carriages, and here the scene became most interesting—the horsemen galloping across the fields to accompany the engine, and the people on foot running on each side of the road, endeavouring in vain to keep up with the cavalcade. The Rail-Way descending with a gentle inclination towards Darlington, though not uniform, the rate of speed was consequently variable. On this part of the Rail-Way it was wished to ascertain at what rate of speed the engine could travel with safety. In some parts the speed was frequently twelve miles per hour, and in one place, for a short distance, near Darlington, fifteen miles per hour; and at that time the number of passengers was counted to four hundred and fifty, which, together with the coals, merchandise, and carriages, would amount to near ninety tons.

After some little delay in arranging the procession, the engine with her load arrived at Darlington, a distance of eight miles and three quarters, in sixty-five minutes, exclusive of stops, averaging about eight miles an hour. Six carriages, loaded with coals, intended for Darlington, were then left behind; and after obtaining a fresh supply of water, and arranging the procession to accommodate a band of music and passengers from Darlington, the engine set off again. Part of the Rail-Way from Darlington to Stockton has little declivity, and in one place is quite level; and as in the upper part, it was intended to try the speed of the engine; in this part it was proposed to prove her capability of dragging a heavy load, and, certainly, the performance excited the astonishment of all present, and exceeded the most sanguine expectations of every one conversant with the subject. The engine arrived at Stockton in three hours and seven minutes after

1

2

leaving Darlington, including stops, the distance being nearly twelve miles, which is at the rate of four miles an hour; and upon the level part of the Rail-Way, the number of passengers in the waggons was counted about five hundred and fifty, and several more clung to the carriages on each side, so that the whole number could not be less than six hundred, which, with the other load, would amount to about eighty

1 A watercolour portrait of George Stephenson, painted in 1836.
2 Locomotive No. 25, the *Derwent*, which went into service in 1845.

tons. Nothing could exceed the beauty and grandeur of the scene. Throughout the whole distance, the fields and lanes were covered with elegantly dressed females, and all descriptions of spectators.

Numerous horses, carriages, gigs, carts, and other vehicles travelled along with the engine, and her immense train of carriages, and in some places within a few yards, without the horses seeming the least frightened; and at one time the passengers by the engine had the pleasure of accompanying and cheering their brother passengers by the stage coach, which passed alongside, and of observing the striking contrast exhibited by the power of the engine and of horses; the engine with her six hundred passengers and load, and the coach with four horses, and only sixteen passengers.

In contemplating the events of the day, either in a national point of view, or as the efforts of a company of individuals furnishing a speedy, efficacious, and certain means of traffic to a wide and extended district, it alike excites the deepest interest and admiration; and the immense train of carriages covered with people, forming a load of from eighty to ninety tons, gliding, as it were, smoothly and majestically along the Rail-Way through files of spectators, at such an astonishing rate of speed, left an impression on those who witnessed it, that will never be forgotten.

Part of the workmen were entertained at Stockton, and part at Yarm, and there was a grand dinner for the proprietors and their more distinguished guests at the Town Hall, in Stockton. Mr. Meynell, of Yarm, was in the chair, and the Mayor of the town acted as vice-president.

LOCOMOTION NO. 1 was the first steam locomotive to run on a public railway but most of the Stockton and Darlington's regular traffic at this time was horse-drawn. The first line built for, and operated solely by, steam haulage was the Liverpool and Manchester Railway.

This project was first discussed in 1822, but opposition to railways was so great that the necessary Act of Parliament was not passed until 1826. George Stephenson, who was appointed Chief Engineer, had considerable difficulties to face in constructing the 31 miles of double line. Apart from tunnels, bridges and viaducts he had to make a way across the marshland of Chat Moss, four miles of bog more than thirty feet in depth.

In 1829, before the line was finished, the directors of the railway held a competition at Rainhill, near Liverpool, to find 'the most improved locomotive engine', laying down strict conditions to which the entrants must conform:

1829 GRAND COMPETITION OF LOCOMOTIVES ON THE LIVERPOOL & MANCHESTER RAILWAY

Stipulations & Conditions on which the Directors of the Liverpool and Manchester Railway offer a Premium of £500 for the most improved locomotive engine.

I. The said Engine must 'effectually consume its own smoke' according to the provisions of the Railway Act, 7th Geo. IV.

II. The Engine, if it weighs six Tons, must be capable of drawing after it, day by day, on a well-constructed Railway, on a level plane, a Train of Carriages of the gross weight of Twenty Tons, including the Tender and Water Tank, at the rate of Ten Miles per Hour, with a pressure of steam in the boiler not exceeding Fifty Pounds on the square inch.

III. There must be Two Safety Valves, one of which must be completely out of the reach or control of the Engine-man, and neither of which must be fastened down while the Engine is working.

IV. The Engine and Boiler must be supported on Springs, and rest on Six Wheels; and the height from the ground to the top of the Chimney must not exceed Fifteen Feet.

V. The weight of the Machine, WITH ITS COMPLEMENT OF WATER in the Boiler, must at most, not exceed Six Tons, and a Machine of less weight will be preferred if it draw AFTER it a PROPORTIONATE weight; and if the weight of the Engine, & c., do not exceed FIVE TONS, then the gross weight to be drawn need not exceed Fifteen Tons; and in that proportion for Machines of still smaller weight — provided that the Engine, & c., shall still be on six wheels, unless the weight (as above) be reduced to Four Tons and a Half, or under, in which case the Boiler, & c., may be placed on four wheels. And the Company shall be at liberty to put the Boiler, Tube, Cylinders, & c., to the test of a pressure of water not exceeding 150 Pounds per square inch, without being answerable for any damage the machine may receive in consequence.

VI. There must be a Mercurial Gauge affixed to the Machine, with Index Rod, showing the Steam Pressure above 45 Pounds per square inch; and constructed to blow out a Pressure of 60 Pounds per inch.

VII. The Engine to be delivered complete for trial, at the Liverpool end of the Railway, not later than the 1st of October next.

VIII. The price of the Engine which may be accepted not to exceed £550, delivered on the Railway; and any Engine not approved to be taken back by the Owner. N. B. — The Railway Company will provide the Engine Tender with a supply of Water and Fuel for the experiment. The distance within the Rails is four feet eight inches and a half.

THE GRAND LOCOMOTIVE COMPETITION

THE 'LIVERPOOL TIMES,' 13th OCTOBER 1829 ON TUESDAY, the first day of trial, the race-ground presented a scene of extraordinary gaiety and bustle. The day being remarkably fine, thousands of persons of all ranks were assembled from the surrounding towns and districts. Upwards of 10,000 persons were computed to have been present, among whom were a greater number of scientific men, and practical engineers, than have been assembled on any previous occasion.

During the whole of the day the different carriages were exhibiting on the Rail-Way, and it is scarcely possible for any one who has not seen them in motion to form any conception of their astonishing speed. In the early part of the day, the carriage of Mr. Robert Stephen-son, of Newcastle, attracted great attention. It ran without any weight attached to it, at the rate of 24 miles in the hour, rushing past the spectators with amazing velocity. It has been stated by several of the papers that it emitted very little smoke; but the fact is, that during the trial it emitted none. Previous to the trial, a little coal was put into it, and then it sent forth a smoke; but after the trial had commenced, it used coke, which as it does not produce any smoke, of course could not emit any. We know that there were some persons on the ground who mistook steam for smoke. After this carriage had moved about for some time, without any weight, cars, containing stones, were attached to it, weighing, together with its own weight, upwards of 17 tons, preparatory to the trial of its speed being made. The precise distance between the point of starting, at or near the weighing shed, to the point of returning, was $1\frac{3}{4}$ mile; but in the adjudication of distances, we are given to understand the judges allowed a furlong at each end for the acquirement and abatement of speed. Our observations apply, however, to the whole distance. With a load of $12\frac{1}{2}$ tons gross, the *Rocket* travelled the above space of $1\frac{3}{4}$ mile, four times forward and backward, equal to 14 miles, in the space of 75 minutes, exclusive of stoppages; but, including the stoppages, the average rate was $10\frac{1}{2}$ miles per hour. In the fifth course, the rate of speed, with a load, augmented by passengers, until equal to 13 tons was full 15 miles an hour.

Mr. Hackworth, of Darlington, ran his carriage along the course during the day; but no trial of its speed with weights took place.

Mr. Winan's machine, worked by two men, and carrying six passengers, was also on the ground. It moved with no great velocity compared to the Locomotive Steam-Carriages, but with considerable speed considering that it was put in motion by human power. One of the

1

2

1 Robert Stephenson's *Rocket* as it appeared at the Rainhill Trials.
2 Timothy Hackworth, an assistant to the Stephensons, subsequently Engine Superintendent of the Stockton and Darlington Railway, who built many fine locomotives.
3 Hackworth's entry for the Rainhill Trials, the *Sans Pareil*.
4 A reproduction of the *Novelty* locomotive incorporating the wheels and one cylinder of the original engine.

3

4

wheels was damaged in the course of the afternoon, by Mr. Hackworth's Locomotive Steam-Carriage.

Mr. Brandreth's horse-power Locomotive Engine exhibited, not in the way of competition, but as exercise. About fifty persons clung round the waggons, giving a gross weight, with the machine, of about 5 tons, and with this weight, the horses (themselves moving scarcely one mile and a quarter an hour) propelled the waggons and load exactly at the rate of five miles an hour.

The engine of Messrs. Braithwaite and Erickson, of London, was universally allowed to exhibit, in appearance and compactness, the beau-ideal of a Locomotive Carriage. Its performance, whilst exercising without a load was most astonishing, passing over a space of $2\frac{3}{4}$ miles in seven minutes and a quarter, including a stop-space of one minute and thirty-three seconds! Had the Rail-Way been completed, the engine would, at this rate, have gone nearly the whole way from Liverpool to Manchester within the hour. Mr. Braithwaite, has, indeed, publicly offered to stake £1000, that as soon as the road is opened, he will perform the entire distance in that time. The velocity with which the *Novelty* moved, surprised and amazed every beholder. It seemed indeed to fly, presenting one of the most sublime spectacles of mechanical ingenuity and human daring the world ever beheld. It actually made one giddy to look at it, and filled the breasts of thousands with lively fears for the safety of the

individuals who were on it, and who seemed not to run along the earth, but to fly, as it were, 'on the wings of the wind.'

On Wednesday Braithwaite and Erickson's carriage drew the weight assigned by the judges, namely, 6 tons 2 cwt., at the rate of $20\frac{3}{4}$ miles per hour. Unfortunately, however, the bellows burst after the first trip, so that the experiment had to be postponed.

The first systematic trial of the power of the engines, under the inspection of the judges, took place on Thursday, when Mr. Stephenson's carriage, the *Rocket*, was brought out to perform the task assigned. This engine has a boiler of a new construction, adapted for coke, the invention of Mr. Henry Booth, the treasurer to the Railway Company. The distance appointed to be run was 70 miles; and it was a condition that, when fairly started, the engine was to travel on the road at a speed of not less than 10 miles per hour, drawing after it a gross weight of 3 tons, for every ton weight of itself. Before starting, the machine was weighed, and the weight ascertained to be 4 tons 5 cwt. the gross weight to be drawn, therefore, was 12 tons 15 cwt., which was accordingly placed behind the engine, part of the said weight consisting of the engine tender, with the needful supply of water and fuel. The prescribed distance of 70 miles, it must be remembered, was to be accomplished by moving backwards and forwards, on a level plane of one mile and three-quarters in length; of course the engine had to pass along this plane 40 times, having

to make as many stops, and each time to regain the lost speed and momentum. She started on her journey about half-past ten in the morning, and performed the first 35 miles in 3 hours and 10 minutes, being upwards of 11 miles an hour. About a quarter of an hour was then consumed in filling the water tank, and obtaining a fresh supply of coke. The second 35 miles were accomplished in less time than the first, being performed in 2 hours and 52 minutes, which is at the rate of upwards of 12 miles an hour, including stoppages, the whole time from the first starting to the final arrival being under six hours and a half. The speed of the carriage over the ground was frequently 18 miles per hour, and sometimes more, and the motion is represented by the gentlemen who accompanied it, as particularly easy and agreable. The engine having to return and stop at the same point so frequently, opportunity was thereby afforded for a considerable number of gentlemen to have the pleasure of a ride; amongst others mounted behind the engine, we noticed Dr. Traill, Mr. Robert Gladstone, Mr. Henry Moss, etc. etc. On the whole, the performance gave great satisfaction, and the work done was far more than the quantum prescribed by the Directors of the Rail-Way.

On saturday morning . . . the *Novelty* with her appointed load, started, and performed the first trip of three miles and a half in good style. On the second journey, however, owing to an accident to one of the pipes, all locomotion was suspended; and before the injury, though unimportant, could be repaired, the day was too far advanced to recommence her allotted task. It was evident, from the frequent, though slight, derangements which had occurred to this engine, that a little further time was desirable before her performance should be again brought under the special notice of the judges. Accordingly, it was arranged by mutual consent that the London engine should run the 70 miles with her load on Wednesday (tomorrow). On the Saturday afternoon, however, the injury sustained being repaired, she appeared again on the course, with the Directors' carriage attached to her, in which were about forty ladies and gentlemen, and with which she moved along in beautiful style at the almost incredible speed of upwards of 30 miles per hour! In the course of the day, Mr. Stephenson's engine also performed an equally brilliant feat. Between the occurrence and the repair of the accident to Messrs. Braithwaite's carriage, that of Mr. Stephenson's the *Rocket*, ran, without load or tender, 7 miles in 14 minutes, which is at the rate of 30 miles an hour; and one of the trips of $3\frac{1}{2}$ miles was performed in 6 minutes and 37 seconds, which is at the rate of 32 miles an hour!

The trials lasted eight days altogether and at the end there was no doubt about it, Stephenson's *Rocket* was the winner, although some people felt that had there been a railway near London where the *Novelty* could have been tried out, and perhaps improved before the Trials, the result might have been different.

On 14th June 1830 a locomotive called the *Arrow* drew the first train from Liverpool to Manchester.

A month earlier, on 3rd May 1830, the Canterbury and Whitstable Railway was opened, to become the first railway on which passenger trains were hauled by steam locomotives. However, while technically the Kent line can claim historic precedence it was only worked by locomotive for the last two miles into Whitstable, the four miles at the Canterbury end being operated by fixed engines. Even then the incline out of Whitstable proved too much for the locomotive and a stationary engine was installed, leaving only a single mile worked by the locomotive.

A TRIP WITH MR. STEPHENSON

described by Fanny Kemble

IN AUGUST 1830 Fanny Kemble was playing at a Liverpool theatre. This famous niece of Sarah Siddons, who married a Philadelphian and fought for the emancipation of the slaves in Georgia, visited the railroad. She wrote to a friend:

My dear Harriet,

A common sheet of paper is enough for love, but a foolscap extra can alone contain a railroad and my ecstasies. There was once a man, who was born at Newcastle-upon-Tyne, who was a common coal-digger! this man had an immense constructiveness, which displayed itself in pulling his watch to pieces and putting it together again; in making a pair of white shoes when he happened to be some days without occupation; finally—here there is a great gap in my story it brought him in the capacity of an engineer before a committee of the House of Commons, with his head full of plans for constructing a railroad from Liverpool to Manchester. It so happened that to the quickest and most powerful perceptions, to the most indefatigable industry and perseverance, and the most accurate knowledge of the phenomena of nature as they affect his peculiar labours, this man joined an utter want of the 'gift of the gab.' He could no more explain to others what he meant to do and how he meant to do it, than he could fly; and therefore the members of the House of Commons, after saying 'There is rock to be excavated to a depth of more than sixty feet, there are embankments to be made nearly to the same height, there is a swamp of five miles in length to be traversed, in which if you drop an iron rod it sinks and disappears: how will you do all this?' and receiving no answer but a broad Northumbrian 'I can't tell you how I'll do it, but I can tell you I will do it,' dismissed Stephenson as a visionary. Having prevailed upon a company of Liverpool gentlemen to be less incredulous, and having raised funds for his great undertaking, in December of 1826 the first spade was struck into the ground.

And now I will give you an account of my yesterday's excursion. A party of sixteen persons was ushered into a large courtyard, where, under cover, stood several carriages of a peculiar construction, one of which was prepared for our reception. It was a long-bodied vehicle with seats placed across it, back to back; the one we were in had six of these benches and was a sort of uncovered char-a-banc. The wheels were placed upon two iron bands, which formed the road, and to which they are fitted, being so constructed as to slide along without any danger of hitching or becoming displaced, on the same principle as a thing sliding on a concave groove. The carriage was set in motion by a mere push, and, having received this impetus, rolled with us down an inclined plane into a tunnel which forms the entrance to the railroad. This tunnel is four hundred yards long (I believe) and will be lighted by gas. At the end of it we emerged from darkness, and, the ground becoming level, we stopped. There is another tunnel parallel with this, only much wider and longer, for it extends from the place which we had now reached, and where the steam-carriages start, and which is quite out of Liverpool, the whole way under the town, to the docks. This tunnel is for waggons and other heavy carriages; and as the engines which are to draw the trains along the railroad do not enter these tunnels, there is a large building at this entrance which is to be inhabited by steam-engines of a stationary turn of mind, and different construction from the travelling ones, which are to propel the trains through the tunnels to the terminus in the town, without going out of their houses themselves. The length of the tunnel parallel

2

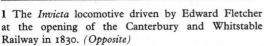
1 The *Invicta* locomotive driven by Edward Fletcher at the opening of the Canterbury and Whitstable Railway in 1830. *(Opposite)*
2 The Moorish arch at Edgehill, the exotic Liverpool entrance to the Liverpool and Manchester Railway, from a print by Ackermann and Co.

to the one we passed through is (I believe) two thousand two hundred yards.

I wonder if you are understanding one word of what I am saying all this while!

We were introduced to the little engine which was to drag us along the rails. She (for they make these curious little firehorses all mares) consisted of a boiler, a stove, a small platform, a bench, and behind the bench a barrel containing enough water to prevent her being thirsty for fifteen miles—the whole machine not bigger than a common fire-engine. She goes upon two pairs of wheels, which are her feet, and are moved by bright steel legs called pistons. These are propelled by steam, and in proportion as more steam is applied to the upper extremities (the hip-joints, I suppose) of these pistons, the faster they move the wheels; and when it is desirable to diminish the speed, the steam, which unless suffered to escape would burst the boiler, evaporates through a safety-valve into the air. The reins, bit, and bridle of this wonderful beast — a small handle which applies or withdraws the steam from its legs or pistons, so that a child could manage it. The coals, which are its oats, were under the bench, and there was a small glass tube affixed to the boiler, with water in it, which indicates by its fullness or emptiness when the creature wants water, which is immediately conveyed to it from its reservoirs. There is a chimney to the stove, but as they burn coke there is none of the dreadful black smoke which accompanies the progress of

a steam-vessel. This snorting little animal, which I felt rather inclined to pat, was then harnessed to our carriage, and, Mr. Stephenson having taken me on the bench of the engine with him, we started at about ten miles an hour.

The steam-horse being ill-adapted for going up and down hill, the road was kept at a certain level, and appeared sometimes to sink below the surface of the earth and sometimes to rise above it. Almost at starting it was cut through the solid rock, which formed a wall on either side of it, about sixty feet high. You can't imagine how strange it seemed to be journeying on thus, without any visible cause of progress other than the magical machine, with its flying white breath and rhythmical, unvarying pace, between these rocky walls, which are already clothed with moss and ferns and grasses. When I reflected that these great masses of stone had been cut asunder to allow our passage thus far below the surface of the earth, I felt as if no fairy tale was ever half so wonderful as what I saw. Bridges were thrown from side to side across the top of these cliffs, and the people looking down upon us from them seemed like pygmies standing in the sky.

I must be more concise, though, or I shall want room. We were to go only fifteen miles, that distance being sufficient to show the speed of the engine and take us to the most beautiful and wonderful object on the road. After proceeding through this rocky defile, we presently found ourselves raised upon embankments ten or twelve feet high. We then came to a moss

2

or swamp of considerable extent, on which no human feet could tread without sinking, and yet it bore the road which bore us. This had been the great stumbling-block in the minds of the committee of the House of Commons, but Mr. Stephenson had succeeded in overcoming it. A foundation of hurdles, or, as he called it, basket-work, was thrown over the morass, and the interstices were filled with moss and other elastic matter. Upon this the clay and soil were laid down and the road does float, for we passed over it at the rate of five and twenty miles an hour, and saw the stagnant swamp trembling on the surface of the soil on either side of us. I hope you understand me. The embankment had gradually been rising higher and higher, and in one place, where the soil was not settled enough to form banks, Stephenson had constructed artificial ones of wood-work, over which the mounds of earth would lie, for he said that though the wood-work would rot, before it did so the banks of earth which covered it would be sufficiently consolidated to support the road.

We had now come fifteen miles and stopped where the road traversed a wide and deep valley. Stephenson made me alight and led me down to the bottom of this ravine, over which, in order to keep his road level, he had thrown a magnificent viaduct of nine arches, the middle one of which is seventy feet high, through which we saw the whole of this beautiful little valley. It was lovely and wonderful beyond all words. Here he told me many curious things respecting this ravine; how he believed the Mersey had once rolled through it; how the soil had proved so unfavourable for the foundations of his bridge that it was built upon piles which had been driven into the earth to an enormous depth; how, while digging for a foundation, he had come to a tree bedded in the earth fourteen feet below the surface of the ground; how tides are caused, and how another flood might be caused; all of which I have remembered and noted down at much greater length than I can here enter upon it. He explained to me the whole construction of the steam-engine, and said he could soon make a famous engineer of me, which, considering the wonderful things he has achieved, I dare not say is impossible. His way of explaining himself is peculiar, but very striking, and I understood, without difficulty, all that he said to me. We then rejoined the rest of the party, and the engine having received its supply of water, the carriage was placed behind it, for it cannot turn, and was set off at its utmost speed, thirty-five miles an hour, swifter than a bird flies (for they tried the experiment with a snipe).

1 *The Tunnel*, from an Ackermann print. Locomotives were not used through the gas-lit tunnel, trains were rope-hauled by a stationary engine.
2 The *Northumbrian* locomotive built by the Stephensons for service on the Liverpool and Manchester Railway in 1831.

1

You cannot conceive what that sensation of cutting the air was; the motion is as smooth as possible too. I could either have read or written; and as it was, I stood up, and with my bonnet off 'drank the air before me.' The wind, which was strong, or perhaps the force of our own thrusting against it, absolutely weighed my eyelids down. When I closed my eyes this sensation of flying was quite delightful, and strange beyond description, yet, strange as it was, I had a perfect sense of security and not the slightest fear. At one time, to exhibit the power of the engine, Mr. Stephenson caused it to be fastened in front of ours; moreover, a waggon laden with timber was also chained to us, and thus propelling the idle steam engine, and dragging the loaded waggon which was beside it, and our own carriage full of people behind, this brave little she-dragon of ours flew on. Farther on she met three carts, which [were] fastened in front of her without the slightest delay or difficulty. When I add that this pretty little creature can run with equal facility either backwards or forwards, I believe I have given you an account of all her capacities.

Now for a word or two about the master of all these marvels, with whom I am most horribly in love. He is a man from fifty to fifty-five years of age. [Stephenson was then forty-nine.] His face is fine, though careworn, and bears an expression of deep thoughtfulness. His mode of explaining his ideas is peculiar and very original, striking, and forcible. Al-

though his accent indicates strongly his north country birth, his language has not the slightest touch of vulgarity or coarseness. He has certainly turned my head.

Four years have sufficed to bring this great undertaking to an end. The railroad will be opened upon the 15th of next month. The Duke of Wellington is coming down to be present on the occasion, and, I suppose, what with the thousands of spectators and the novelty of the spectacle, there will never have been a scene of more striking interest. The whole cost of the work (including the engine and carriages) will have been eight hundred and thirty thousand pounds. It is already worth double that sum. The directors have kindly offered us three places for the opening, which is a great favour, for people are bidding almost anything for a place, I understand!

Fanny managed to break her tour to return for the opening by the Duke of Wellington and described the occasion in another letter.

1 Goods trains and a second-class passenger train on the Liverpool and Manchester Railway, from prints published by the Ackermann Company in 1831-3.
2 The scene at Edgehill at the opening of the railway on 15th September 1830.

THE OPENING OF LIVERPOOL AND MANCHESTER RAILWAY

described by Fanny Kemble

WE STARTED [from Liverpool] on Wednesday last, to the number of about eight hundred people. The most intense curiosity and excitement prevailed. Though the weather was uncertain, enormous crowds of densely packed people lined the road, shouting and waving hats and handkerchiefs as we flew by them. What with the sight and sound of these cheering multitudes and the tremendous velocity with which we were borne past them, my spirits rose to the true champagne height, and I never enjoyed anything so much as the first hour of our progress.

I had been unluckily separated from my mother in the first distribution of places, but by an exchange of seats which she was enabled to make she rejoined me when I was at the height of my ecstasy, which was considerably dampened by finding that she was frightened to death, and intent upon nothing but devising means of escaping from a situation which appeared to her to threaten with instant annihilation herself and all her travelling companions.

While I was chewing the cud of this disappointment, which was rather bitter, as I had expected her to be as delighted as myself with our excursion, a man flew by us, calling out through a speaking trumpet to stop the engine, for that somebody in the directors' carriage had sustained an injury. We were all stopped accordingly, and presently a hundred voices were heard exclaiming that Mr. Huskisson was killed. The confusion that ensued is indescribable: the calling out from carriage to carriage to ascertain the truth, the contrary reports which were sent back to us, the hundred questions eagerly uttered at once, and the repeated and urgent demands for surgical assistance, created a sudden turmoil that was quite sickening. At last we distinctly ascertained that the unfortunate man's thigh was broken.

From Lady Wilton, who was in the Duke's carriage, and within three yards of the spot where the accident happened, I had the following details, the horror of witnessing which we were spared through our situation behind the great carriage. The engine had stopped to take in a supply of water, and several of the gentlemen in the directors' carriage had jumped out to look about them. Lord Wilton, Count Batthyany, Count Matuscewitz, and Mr. Huskisson among the rest were standing talking on the middle of the road, when an engine on the other line, which was parading up and down merely to show its speed, was seen coming down upon them like lightning. The most active of those in peril sprang back into their seats. Lord Wilton saved his life only by rushing behind the Duke's [Wellington's] carriage, and Count Matuscewitz had but just leaped into it, with the engine all but touching his heels as he did so. Poor Mr. Huskisson, less active from the effects of age and ill health, bewildered too, by the frantic cries of 'Stop the engine! Clear the track!' that resounded on all sides, completely lost his head, looked helplessly to the right and left, and was instantaneously prostrated by the fatal machine, which dashed down like a thunderbolt upon him, and passed over his

2

leg, smashing and mangling it in the most horrible way. (Lady Wilton said she distinctly heard the crushing of the bone.) So terrible was the effect of the appalling incident that, except for that ghastly 'crushing' and poor Mr. Huskisson's piercing shriek, not a sound was heard or a word uttered among the immediate spectators of the catastrophe.

Lord Wilton was the first to raise the poor sufferer, and calling to aid his surgical skill, which is considerable, he tied up the severed artery, and for a time, at least, prevented death by loss of blood. Mr. Huskisson was then placed in a carriage with his wife and Lord Wilton, and the engine, having been detached from the directors' carriage, conveyed them to Manchester.

So great was the shock produced upon the whole party by this event that the Duke of Wellington declared his intention not to proceed, but return immediately to Liverpool. However, upon its being represented to him that the whole population of Manchester had turned out to witness the procession, and that a disappointment might give rise to riots and disturbances, he consented to go on, and gloomily enough the rest of the journey was accomplished.

One Manchester man saw in the opening of the railway to Liverpool the beginning not only of economic but of political change. He wrote:

'Parliamentary Reform must follow soon after the opening of this road. A million of persons will pass over it in the course of this year, and see that hitherto unseen village of Newton; and they must be convinced of the absurdity of its sending two members to Parliament whilst Manchester sends none.'

During the years that followed, Britain became covered with a network of railways. Between 1825 and 1835 fifty-four Railway Acts were passed through Parliament — one of them for Robert Stephenson's London and Birmingham line. In the next two years thirty-nine received the royal assent, and then again in 1844—47 there was another boom in railway building. Through these arteries the development of industry was hastened and much of Britain changed from a rural to an urban society.

1 Parkside Station, where Mr. Huskisson's fatal accident took place.
2 Viaduct across the Sankey Valley, Lancashire.
3 The entrance to the railway at Edgehill, Liverpool. (2) and (3) drawn by T. T. Bury and published by Ackermann and Co. in 1831.

2

1

1 A view of the railway across Chat Moss.
2 The excavation of Olive Mount, four miles from
Liverpool. Both from Ackermann prints drawn by
T. T. Bury and engraved by H. Pyall.
3 A view of the Manchester and Liverpool Railway
taken at Newton in 1885, drawn by Calvert, aquatint
by Havell.

2

3

THE WORLD ADOPTS THE RAILWAY

THE SUCCESS of the Liverpool and Manchester Railway gave encouragement to railway enthusiasts elsewhere. More and more railways were built in Britain: the Leicester and Swannington, the Grand Junction Railway, the London and Birmingham, and in Scotland lines from Monkland to Kirkintilloch and from Glasgow to Garnkirk; and overseas the lines began to appear.

Steam locomotion was first introduced to France in 1832 on a mine railway which had been opened in 1823. The Dublin and Kingstown Railway in Ireland was opened in 1834. The same year the Belgian Government began construction of a line from Brussels to Malines which was opened in 1835 with two locomotives built by Stephenson. In December 1835

Der Adler, another Stephenson locomotive, opened the Ludwigsbahn from Nuremberg to Fürth.

A line from St. Petersburg to Pavlovsk was opened in 1837, although later development in Russia was slow. That year, too, the first steam locomotive, sent out from England, began work on the Kaiser Ferdinands Nordbahn near Vienna, though Austria had had horse railways since 1832.

In Holland a line from Amsterdam to Haarlem was opened on 24th September 1839 and ten days later five miles of line from Naples to Portici were opened in Italy. The first railway in Scandinavia, a privately owned line from Copenhagen to Roskilde, did not come until 1847 and railways in Norway and

3

4

1 The first locomotive in Costa Rica.
2 American express trains, from a lithograph by Currie and Ives.
3 The opening of the Glasgow and Garnkirk Railway.
4 The *Buddicombe* locomotive which was in use on French railways in 1854.

1

2

3

4

5

1—8 (1) Austria's oldest locomotive, the *Ajax*, was built by James Turner Evans at Newton. It first ran between Floridsdorf and Stokerau in July 1841. (2) An early Swedish train. (3) *La Belge*, built for the Belgian State Railway in 1835. (4) The opening of the Ludwigsbahn (from a painting). (5) Japanese print showing the railway at Takanawa in 1880. (6) Built by Stephenson, this locomotive was among the first imported into New South Wales in 1855. (7) A Fairlie type locomotive in use on the Port Chalmers Railway, New Zealand, in 1872. (8) Students inspecting a modern Chinese train. The Chinese Government of 1876 did not like railways but the People's Republic is today engaged on an enormous railway building programme.

Sweden did not appear until the next decade — and in Finland not until 1862.

Switzerland, which since 1844 had had a mile-long extension of the Alsace Railway linking Basle with the French frontier, built a line between Zürich and Baden in 1847. In 1849 Robert Stephenson was called in to advise on the country's railway development.

In 1848 the first Spanish line, from Barcelona to Mataró, was inaugurated with a ceremony, attended by the full court, at which the Cardinal Archbishop of Toledo blessed the locomotive.

As the rails spread across the Continent the European powers built railways in their overseas possessions. Indeed there was a railway in Cuba eleven years before the first line in Spain. In India there was strong pressure in favour of using waterways for communications, but railways were developed from 1853.

For Australia the British Government recommended a standard gauge of 4 ft. $8\frac{1}{2}$ in. but in 1852 and 1853 New South Wales and Victoria went ahead with lines on a 5 ft. 3 in. gauge. The next year New South Wales converted to 4 ft. $8\frac{1}{2}$ in. Later Queensland and Western Australia built lines at 3 ft. 6 in. — and South Australia had all three gauges! The result, still with us, is that travellers across Australia must change trains as they pass from state to state.

In New Zealand the Lyttelton and Christchurch Railway was commenced in 1860 to a gauge of 5 ft. 3 in. but an Act of Parliament in 1870 set down a gauge of 3 ft. 6 in. for all future railways, thereby preventing the confusion which grew up in Australia.

In Africa, Egypt's first railway dated from 1852, and at the other end of the Continent the first line, two miles long from Durban to the Point, opened in 1860. In 1862 the first steam trains began to run in South Africa between Cape Town and Eerste, and after the discovery of diamonds in 1867 the railway system grew rapidly.

Japan's first railway, between Yokohama, Tokyo and Shimbashi, was not opened until 1872; and the first railway in China, a nine-mile line from Shanghai to Woosung, begun in 1876, was torn up by the authorities — although four years later another line was opened.

6

7

8

PIONEERS IN AMERICA

AS EARLY as 1764 there was a cable-operated tramway of grooved logs in operation in the United States at Lewiston, New York, where it hauled supplies for a military camp. Other similar tramways followed, including, in 1826, the horse-hauled Granite Railway in Quincey, Massachusetts. The wooden track of this railway was iron faced. Some people claim that this should be considered the 'first railroad in the United States'.

While Richard Trevithick was demonstrating his first locomotive in Europe, inventors were also at work in America. Oliver Evans, a Philadelphia blacksmith, was commissioned to build a dredge, but it ended up as a steam-operated dredge plus wheels and a propeller—the first steam-powered amphibious craft—which he called his *Orukter Amphibolos*. Unfortunately, when it set out on the cobbled streets of Philadelphia the axles and the wheels collapsed.

The first steam locomotive to run on tracks in the United States was built by Colonel John Stevens, a farsighted advocate of railways who, in 1812, published a paper entitled *Documents relating to the superior advantage of Railways over Canal Navigation*. In 1825 he built a circular track with a racked rail on his estate at Hoboken, New Jersey. On this track his locomotive reached a speed of twelve miles per hour carrying six passengers.

Although Stevens, by this time seventy-six, made no further active contribution to American railroad history, his demonstrations stimulated the interest of others. Among them was John Jervis, chief engineer of the Delaware and Hudson Canal Company. In 1828 his company built a nine-mile stretch of horse-operated track between their mines and the end of their canal at Honesdale, Pennsylvania. The same year Jervis sent his assistant, Horatio B. Allen, to England, where he was a witness of the Rainhill Trials. Allen was commissioned to purchase locomotives for the company.

One of them, the *Stourbridge Lion*, arrived in New York in May 1829 and was tried out at Honesdale on 8th August 1829 with Allen at the controls. A festive crowd turned up for the occasion and a cannon was fired for the official start (overcharged, it tore the arm off the man who discharged it). The locomotive, with a red and gold lion's head on the front of the boiler, weighed nearly eight tons—five tons more than had been thought at the time of its purchase.

Three hundred yards from the start the track crossed a rickety trestle bridge thirty feet above Lackawaxen Creek. Allen took it at full speed, twenty miles an hour, and reached the other side. Three miles farther on he reversed and came back to the start. The *Lion* had proved itself, but it was immediately decided that it was too heavy for the track and its active life was brought to a rapid close.

The following year a one-horse-power engine, called *Tom Thumb*, was tried out on the Baltimore and Ohio Railroad and hauled a car-load of thirty-six people at a maximum speed of eighteen miles per hour.

British engineers had advised that the curves

1

2

3

4

1 Evans's *Orukter Amphibolos*.
2 The *Best Friend of Charleston*.
3 John Stevens's Experimental Railway.
4 The *Stourbridge Lion*, built by Poster and Rastrick.
5 Peter Cooper's *Tom Thumb* (1829-30).
6 The *Atlantic* locomotive.

of the Baltimore and Ohio's track, which included one on a 150-foot radius, made it impossible to use steam power on the railroad. Shareholders began to withdraw. Peter Cooper, a man who had bought land along the track, was worried about his own investment. As he told it later in the *Boston Herald*, the directors of the railroad 'had a fit of the blues. I had naturally a knack of contriving, and I told the

5

6

directors I believed I could knock together a locomotive that would get around that curve . . .

'So I came to New York and got a bit of an engine, about one horse-power (three and one-half cylinder and fourteen-inch stroke), and carried it back to Baltimore.'

Cooper added a boiler and set his engine up on wheels—and it worked. The trial on 28th August 1830 attracted little attention in the press, but it perturbed the local stage-coach operators. The largest firm challenged Cooper to a race. On a double track their finest grey was set against the *Tom Thumb*.

The horse soon had the lead, but the loco-motive built up power and speed and overtook the horse. It was well ahead when the belt which operated the fan for the fire slipped from its pulley. As the steam pressure fell the speed of the locomotive dropped, and the horse came galloping past to win, to the delight of the supporters of the horse-drawn train. But their jubilation did not prevent the Baltimore and Ohio directors from deciding to adopt steam power. As far as they were concerned the little *Tom Thumb* had amply proved itself.

Like the Liverpool and Manchester Railway in Britain the company announced a compe-tition for a steam engine, which was won in 1831 by the *Atlantic*, the first 'grasshopper'-type locomotive, built at York, Pennsylvania, by Phineas Davis.

Late in 1829, Horatio Allen, driver of the *Lion*, took charge of the building of a railroad

3

for the South Carolina Canal and Railroad Company. The seaport of Charleston saw how the Baltimore and Ohio line would increase Baltimore's trade at their expense, and so planned a railway of its own.

Allen ordered two locomotives to be built by the West Point Foundry in New York City, and this railroad can claim to be the first in the United States built expressly for steam locomotion. The first locomotive, named *The Best Friend of Charleston,* arrived by sea in October and, after undergoing trials, drew the first train out of Charleston on Christmas Day 1830. Behind the locomotive was a flat wagon with a detachment of artillerymen and the cannon used to signal the opening, then came two covered coaches full of celebrities and dignitaries. Great crowds came to watch, and there were bands and fireworks.

The locomotive gave excellent service for six months, then one day her fireman shut off the safety valve and the boiler exploded, making an end of him and of his *Best Friend.* To dispel the fears this incident put in passengers' heads the line thereafter placed a flat car piled with bales of cotton immediately behind the locomotive. The cotton was to shield the passengers should a similar accident occur.

The makers of *The Best Friend* supplied the first locomotive, the *De Witt Clinton,* for the Mohawk and Hudson Railroad. A charter for the railroad had been given in 1826, but various delays prevented the completion of the seventeen-mile track until 1831.

On the inauguratory trip the passengers came under a rain of smoke, sparks and cinders from the chimney stack. Those in the open carriages protected themselves with their umbrellas — only to find that the umbrella covers disappeared in flames. Soon the passengers found their clothes were on fire and most of them spent the journey trying to put each other out! However, not one person who set out failed to complete both the outward and the return journeys.

Within ten years of the opening of these first American railroads there were nearly three thousand miles of track in operation in the United States, and by the outbreak of the Civil War the total had increased tenfold. Unfortunately, these lines were not to a standard gauge, which made through traffic impossible.

A RAILWAY COAST TO COAST

IN 1835 Senator Chase of Ohio introduced a Bill to the United States Congress to provide a survey of four routes for a railroad to link the nation from coast to coast; Jefferson Davis, Secretary of War, initiated reconnaissance for five other routes; and two years later Stephen A. Douglas promoted another Bill to provide three further routes—but, though interest and speculation was considerable and much research was done, no positive action was taken to build a railroad to link the eastern and western states of the United States.

In 1861 the beginning of the Civil War made clear the vulnerability of the nearly isolated west coast. It was national defence, rather than anything else, that led to the passing of the Enabling Act, signed by Abraham Lincoln

help finance the railway. The railway received a strip of land, 130 yards wide, along its whole length, and in addition a further grant of 3,000 acres of land, to be freely selected by the railway authorities within ten miles of the tracks, was made for every mile of line. There was still difficulty in raising money and by Act of 2nd July 1864 Lincoln doubled the land grants.

There was disagreement from the start. The engineers thought that the line should connect with a 4 ft. $8\frac{1}{2}$ in. gauge line east of Missouri, but California already had a five-foot gauge railway. Lincoln supported their demand for a five-foot gauge on the new line, but Congress prescribed the standard gauge. (In the circumstances Congress was right, but if the choice

on 1st July 1862, which created the 'Union Pacific Railroad Company, authorising it to 'lay out, construct, furnish and maintain and enjoy a continuous railroad and telegraph line, with the appurtenances, from a point on the 100th meridian of longitude west from Greenwich between the south margin of the valley of the Republican river and the north margin of the valley of the Platte in the Territory of Nebraska to the western boundary of Nevada Territory.'

The Act also provided for a connection between a point on the western boundary of the state of Iowa and the 100th meridian, and provided for land grants and bond issues to

1 A construction train for the trans-American railway. The workers lived in, and on top of, the long cars which were also used as store rooms for food and dining cars. The train moved forward as building progressed.
2 Track-laying in Wyoming.
THE TRANSCONTINENTAL LINE TODAY
3 A diesel freight train of the Union Pacific Railroad in the Columbia River Gorge, Oregon.
4 Southern Pacific streamliner *Golden State* near Picacho Peak, Arizona.

3

1

2

could be made today a wide gauge would probably be chosen.)

The first sod was cut at Sacramento, California on 22nd February 1863. But in the east there were more complications. Lincoln had specified a place called Council Bluffs, across river from Omaha, as the Missouri railhead. The engineers preferred Bellevue, a few miles farther south, and started construction there. $100,000 had been spent before the President forced them to stop. Construction from Council Bluffs began on 2nd December 1863, but the first rail was not laid until July 1865. The task was formidable. Raw materials, including 6,250 sleepers and 50,000 tons of rails, had to be carried over hundreds of miles from the east by ox cart, or by boat up the Missouri River.

As the railway grew the rails were brought up to the end of the line on an open truck drawn by two horses, which were then unhitched and a single small horse used. A crew of five men stood on each side of the track. At a command from the foreman each crew seized a rail from the back of the truck, pulled it out to its full length and, at the foreman's shout of 'Down,' placed it on the sleepers. A man at the far end checked and adjusted the width between the rails and the horse moved forward pulling the truck over the newly laid rail, the process being repeated until the load of thirty rails had all been laid. Following close behind the layers came the teams who spiked the rails to the sleepers. An average of two miles was laid each day.

When they reached the plains the construction teams came under Indian attack. The Indians were right in seeing the railroad as an enemy. It opened up new territory and made possible the extinction of the bison herds, destroying the Indians' hunting grounds and rapidly leading to their confinement in reservations. But the Indians made pioneering a railroad a dangerous occupation.

The construction gangs had to take everything they needed with them, and every few miles a new 'end of track' town sprang up, complete with saloons and gambling houses operated by hangers-on who saw an easy way of making money out of the isolated railroad men. This travelling community was given the name of 'Hell on Wheels', and at one stage got so rough that the army at Fort D. A. Russell in Wyoming was called in to restore order. The entire 'population' was run out of town and only permitted to return when arrangements had been made to ensure that in future the community would be orderly.

In 1867 the line reached an altitude of 8,247 feet at Sherman Hill as it crossed the Rocky

1 Australia today: a double-headed diesel passenger train of the Victorian State Railways.
2 The *Orange Express* near Brandfort, Orange Free State, South Africa.
3 Sunday on the Union Pacific Railway about 1875.
4 Dale Creek Bridge in Wyoming was built of timber and later replaced by a 'spider web' bridge of steel, only to be abandoned for a more direct route.

Mountains. Meanwhile the Central Pacific Company was following the watercourses up the western slopes of the Sierra Nevada. Originally it had been planned that they should only build the line as far as the boundary of California, but permission was obtained to continue eastward to meet the other company and they pressed on across Nevada to the Great Salt Lake.

Both companies pushed forward, eager for the grants of land that more line built would give. They met early in 1869 in Western Utah, but neither company would acknowledge the fact. Both went on building line at speed. Congress debated ways of stopping this pointless competition. After 225 miles of double track had been laid agreement was reached and the link was made on 10th May 1869.

The ceremony opened with a prayer, then the spikes of silver and gold and a special sleeper, which were to be used for the formal completion of the line, were presented and all except the final golden spike were driven home.

Governor Sandford, the President of Central Pacific, raised his maul, which had been wired so that by telegraph its blows would ring the fire alarm of the Tower in San Francisco and the bell of the Capitol in Washington, signalling to all America that the railway was complete. Governor Sandford struck; and missed, as did Dr. Durant who struck the next blow. Other guests were invited to tap the spike and it fell into place in the hole bored for it.

Two locomotives, *Jupiter* and 119, were unhooked from their trains and moved forward until their cowcatchers touched and bottles of champagne were broken. Then, hooked up again, the trains took it in turns to cross the rails. The ceremonial spikes and sleeper were then quickly removed and replaced by conventional materials; but the new sleeper was soon torn to pieces by souvenir hunters, and half a dozen more—and two rails—had to be replaced in the next six months.

1 An early poster advertising the transcontinental route.
2 The scene at Promontory, Utah, on 10th May 1869. The railroad is complete — shaking hands in the centre are Mr. Montague (left), Chief Engineer of the Central Pacific and Mr. Dodge (right), Chief Engineer of the Union Pacific Railroad.
3 *Across the Continent,* a Currier and Ives lithograph (1868).

ACROSS THE PLAINS

I MADE MY OBSERVATORY on the top of a fruit-waggon, and sat by the hour upon that perch to spy about me, and to spy in vain for something new. It was a world almost without a feature; an empty sky, an empty earth; front and back, the line of railway stretched from horizon to horizon, like a cue across a billiard-board; on either hand, the green plain ran till it touched the skirts of heaven.

Along the track innumerable wild sunflowers, no bigger than a crown-piece, bloomed in a continuous flowerbed; grazing beasts were seen upon the prairie at all degrees of distance and diminution; and now and again we might perceive a few dots beside the railroad which grew more and more distinct as we drew nearer till they turned into wooden cabins, and then dwindled and dwindled in our wake until they melted into their surroundings, and we were once more alone upon the billiard-board. The train toiled over this infinity like a snail; and being the one thing moving, it was wonderful what huge proportions it began to assume in our regard. It seemed miles in length, and either end of it within but a step of the horizon. Even my own body or my own head seemed a great thing in that emptiness. I note the feeling the more readily as it is the contrary of what I have read of in the experience of others. Day and night, above the roar of the train, our ears were kept busy with the incessant chirp of grasshoppers—a noise like the winding up of countless clocks and watches,

which began after a while to seem proper to that land.

To one hurrying through by steam there was a certain exhilaration in this spacious vacancy, this greatness of the air, this discovery of the whole arch of heaven, this straight, unbroken, prison-line of the horizon.

Although it was chill, I was obliged to open my window, for the degradation of the air soon became intolerable to one who was awake and using the full supply of life. Outside, in a glimmering night, I saw the black, amorphous hills shoot by unweariedly into our wake. They that long for morning have never longed for it more earnestly than I.

And yet when day came, it was to shine upon the same broken and unsightly quarter of the world. Mile upon mile, and not a tree, a bird, or a river. Only down the long, sterile canyons, the train shot hooting and awoke the resting echo. That train was the one piece of life in all the deadly land; it was the one actor, the one spectacle fit to be observed in this paralysis of man and nature. And when I think how the railroad has been pushed through this unwatered wilderness and haunt of savage tribes and now will bear an emigrant for some £12 from the Atlantic to the Golden Gates, how at each stage of the construction, roaring, impromptu cities, full of gold and lust and death, sprang up and then died away

again, and are now but wayside stations in the desert; how in these uncouth places pigtailed Chinese pirates worked side by side with border ruffians and broken men from Europe, talking together in a mixed dialect, mostly oaths, gambling, drinking, quarrelling and murdering like wolves; how the plumed hereditary lord of all America heard, in this last fastness, the scream of the 'bad medicine waggon' charioting his foes; and then when I go on to remember that all this epical turmoil was conducted by gentlemen in frock coats, and with a view to nothing more extraordinary than a fortune and a subsequent visit to the one typical achievement of the age in which we live, as if it brought together into one plot all the ends of the world and all the degrees of social rank, and offered to some great writer the busiest, the most extended, and the most varied subject for an enduring literary work. If it be romance, if it be contrast, if it be heroism that we require, what was Troy town to this? But, alas! it is not these things that are necessary —it is only Homer.

Here also we are grateful to the train, as to some god who conducts us swiftly through these shades and by so many hidden perils. Thirst, hunger, the sleight and ferocity of Indians are all no more feared, so lightly do we skim these horrible lands; as the gull, who wings safely through the hurricane and past the shark.

FROM 'ACROSS THE PLAINS'
BY ROBERT LOUIS STEVENSON.

RAILWAYS ACROSS THE CONTINENTS

IN 1870 a start was made on a railway from Callao, in Peru, across the highlands of Oraya to the navigable part of the Amazon, which would link the Pacific and Atlantic coasts of South America. The railway itself was only a small part of the route, most of which would have been by water, but the difficulties in building it were considerable, for the line had to cross the Andean Cordillera.

The mountains rose sheer above deep valleys to sharp ridges and pointed peaks, and it took all the skill of the engineer, the heroic pioneer Henry Meiggs, to find a route. He blasted his way along the mountainside, and when he could go no farther doubled back and zigzagged higher. He used two hundred and fifty tons of dynamite every month and in one ten-mile stretch alone had to drill out fifty tunnels.

When the line reached 6,000 feet a fever epidemic broke out among the crews. When, in 1877, it had reached an altitude of 12,000 feet Meiggs himself died, worn out. The cost of the line over those seven years was 7,000 dead from a labour force of 8,000—a high price to pay.

Fourteen years later the line was completed. At an altitude of 15,694 feet the Galera Tunnel, the highest in the world, was driven through the mountains. Because of the rarefied air it was only possible to work for about three hours a day.

Farther south in Chile and Bolivia the line between Antofagasta and La Paz reaches a height of 13,000 feet. The 729-mile journey takes about forty-eight hours. The line between La Paz and Arica, part of which is racked, has the highest station in the world—General Lagos, at an altitude of 13,900 feet.

On all these routes trains have to be stopped for a time around 7,000 feet to enable passen-

1 Cheyenne Indians, led by Tall Bull, attack a hand-car crew near Fossil Creek, Kansas, on 28th May 1869.
2 Shooting buffaloes in the far west in 1871.
3 The Marquis Viaduct on the Valparaiso and Santiago Railway, 120 ft. high and 600 ft. in length.
4 The line of the Canadian Pacific Railway penetrates the prairies south of Moose Jaw Amulet, Saskatchewan.
5 Driving in the golden spike on the Canadian Pacific Railway, 7th November 1885.

gers not used to the rarefied air to get accustomed to it.

In 1871 a promise of a transcontinental line played a major part in the creation of the modern Dominion of Canada, for the building of such a line was one of the conditions on which British Columbia and the Maritime Provinces insisted before agreeing to enter the confederation. The Intercolonial Railway to the East was completed by 1876. The Pacific Line, although started in 1874, was so delayed that British Columbia talked of secession. In 1880 the building of the line was taken over by the Canadian Pacific Company, and it was completed in 1885. The engineering achievement not only involved the conquest of the Rockies but meant taking

the line across the swamps north of Lake Superior, which sucked up an immeasurable quantity of trees and rock. Even when the line was finally laid across them, sleepers forty feet long had to be used to spread the load. Two other trans-Canadian railways grew out of the Grand Trunk Railway and the Northern Railway. Both are now part of the Canadian National system.

The longest railway journey in the world is from Moscow to Vladivostock on the Trans-Siberian Railway, a distance equivalent to that between London and the tip of Africa.

As early as 1851 the Governor of Eastern Siberia had suggested that a road (on which a railway could later be laid) should be built to link his territories with European Russia,

but it was not until March 1891 that the construction of the line was authorised by Tsar Alexander III. His son, Tsarevich Nicholas, was made chairman of the construction committee. 'The fulfilment of this essential peaceful work,' he said, '. . . is my sacred duty and my sincere desire. I hope to complete the construction of the Siberian line and to have it done cheaply and—most important of all—quickly and solidly.'

Construction began from Vladivostock, in the east, in May 1891 and from Chelyabinsk, in the Urals 4,627 miles away, in July 1892. Materials for the Pacific end of the line had to be shipped right round Asia via the Suez Canal or right round Africa as well. In the west the great Siberian rivers could be used for transportation—during those months of the year when they were not frozen over. Cold, rain, disease and shortage of labour all slowed down what was already a superhuman task of engineering. West of Lake Baikal alone eight massive bridges over 1,000 feet wide had to be built, including ones of 2,800 feet, 2,670 feet and 2,100 feet. They had solid masonry piers and metal spans. When the line reached Lake Baikal the construction of the railway around the lake was postponed, and a combined ferry-boat and ice-breaker was ordered from Britain to carry trains across. The dismantled vessel was delivered in six months, but it was two years later before it was assembled on the lake. The section of line which circled the Manchurian border was not built as planned, because under the Russo-Chinese treaty of 1896 China allowed a more direct route to be constructed through Manchurian territory. However, after the Russo-Japanese war work on the original section was begun, but it was not completed until 1916.

1 *The Countess of Dufferin,* the Canadian Pacific Railway's first locomotive.
2 A modern Trans-Siberian train in the station at Tomsk.
3 This length of track in the Canadian Rockies enters a spiral tunnel at the opening far left and emerges where the train is seen on the right.
4 A church service in Siberia in 1906. Church carriages were part of Trans-Siberian trains.
5 An Australian transcontinental train crossing the Nullarbor Plain near Woomera.
6 Platelaying on the new Soroti to Lira line, Uganda.

Supplies to Russian forces during that war were held up at the Lake Baikal bottle-neck because the ferry could only carry three trains each way daily. As a remedy rails were laid across the ice of the lake itself and wagons hauled across by horses. When the line around the lake was finally completed a ledge had to be cut into the side of the lake, and in one forty-two-mile stretch thirty-eight tunnels had to be bored through the rock.

The Trans-Siberian Railway was a great stimulus to the opening-up of Siberia. Between 1887 and 1892 about 40,000 colonists moved east each year. In 1896 this figure had risen to 200,000.

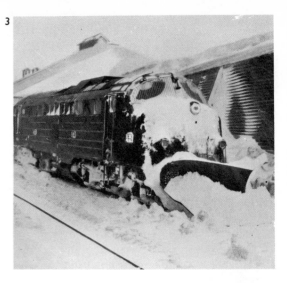

A transcontinental railway was one of the inducements held out to Western Australia to encourage the state to join the Australian Federation, but it was not until 1911 that the work was authorised by the Commonwealth Parliament. The first sod was turned on 14th September 1912, and track-laying commenced in 1913. Most of the construction work was done during the First World War, but, despite shortages of materials, the Commonwealth Railways of Australia had completed the whole line from Kalgoorlie to Port Augusta within four years, and the first passenger train was run on 22nd October 1917.

The building of the Trans-Australian line

did not involve great engineering difficulties, there were no mountains or rivers, and most of the way is a level plain—a flat, waterless desert. In the whole 1,051 miles of the route there is not a single running stream. Wells, bores and reservoirs had to be built at enormous cost for all water requirements. Until the change in recent years to diesel-electric operation this meant that water and coal for locomotives had to be stored along the line, and the railway administration still has to supply the needs of all its staff. A supply train known as the 'Tea and Sugar' operates along the whole line, providing continual fresh supplies of meat, fruit, vegetables, bread, groceries, clothing and household goods. Drinking and domestic water and firewood are carried to areas where they are not obtainable locally—water is carried up to 537 miles.

The Trans-Australian Railway includes the longest stretch of straight railway track in the world. For three hundred miles the line continues, without a single curve, across the dry, treeless Nullarbor Plain.

The building of each great transcontinental line has been a tremendous achievement but short routes can pose equal difficulties. Railway engineers have continually achieved

1 Headed by a diesel-electric locomotive, the inauguratory train leaves the Rimutaka Tunnel, New Zealand. Five and a half miles long, it eliminated the 1 in 15 Rimutaka Incline which was worked on the Fell system.
2 The *Orange Express* passes through Shonweni Gorge, Natal.
3 A diesel locomotive clears its own way on the Bergen Railway, Norway, and helps to stop drifts from forming on the line.
4 A snow-plough at work in northern Scotland.
5 A treble-rotor snow-plough at work on the Orenburg Railway, U.S.S.R. These machines can clear snow up to 6 feet deep.

the impossible. Tunnels have been built with fantastic accuracy. As long ago as 1857 the Mont Cenis Tunnel between Italy and France, $7\frac{1}{2}$ miles long, was built without the aid of dynamite or gelignite, with no horizontal error and with a vertical divergence of only 11.8 inches. Sometimes a way has been made where none existed—as in the Feather River Canyon in the Californian Sierra Nevada, originally thought of as a route for the Central Pacific Railway. For 150 miles this perpendicular cleft cuts its way through the mountains. The torrent at its bottom rises forty-six feet above its normal level when the snow melts in the spring. Experts said it was madness to try to build a railway there, but surveyors worked out routes which gradually reduced the planned gradient from 1 in 43 to 1 in 81. Eventually the Western Pacific's line was built, at fantastic cost, with a gradient of only 1 in 100. To achieve this a ledge 75 miles long was blasted from the solid rock.

Ravines, swamps, deserts, rivers—all are crossed. The Copper River and North West Railroad in Alaska is even laid across a glacier, though one which has not been known to move in living memory. In building this line a bridge was built near to the end of Child Glacier. With the aid of steam jets piles were sunk through the ice of the frozen Copper River. With the bridge already partly built, an unexpected thaw set the glacier moving and its three-mile-wide, 500-feet-high face began to calve iceblocks which threatened to destroy the bridge. The builders fought to keep the piles in place and repair the damage as fast as it was done, and the bridge was saved.

It is not only the physical features of a terrain which set problems for the engineer, whether in building or maintaining his railway. Snow can block the line and avalanches carry with them track and trains. Snow-sheds are built to carry the danger over them, snow-fences sometimes used to deflect the snow and prevent drifts building up on the line. Rain and floods can wash away embankments and bridges; in mountainous country rock falls can be a danger; in deserts sandstorms can bury the track. Animals can prove dangerous too. Teams building the railway from Mombasa to Kisumu on Lake Victoria were continually attacked by man-eating lions. Herds of buffalo often held up trains crossing the American prairies in pioneer days, but small animals can sometimes do worse damage. In Norway the burrowing teledu undermines the permanent way to such an extent that repair teams have to go out and repair the tracks each spring. A swarm of locusts can stop a train; killed or knocked senseless by their impact with the locomotive they are crushed upon the rails to form a mushy pulp which stops the wheels from getting a grip upon the track.

Heat, cold and disease have all taken their heavy toll of the construction gangs who have built our railways. Engineers and maintenance gangs still fight a constant battle against Nature to keep the permanent way open.

NIGHT MAIL

This is the night mail crossing the border,
Bringing the cheque and the postal order,
Letters for the rich, letters for the poor,
The shop at the corner and the girl next door,
Pulling up Beattock, a steady climb —
The gradient's against her but she's on time.

Past cotton grass and moorland boulder,
Shovelling white steam over her shoulder,
Snorting noisily as she passes
Silent miles of wind-bent grasses;
Birds turn their heads as she approaches,
Stare from the bushes at her blank-faced coaches;
Sheepdogs cannot turn her course
They slumber on with paws across,
In the farm she passes no one wakes,
But a jug in a bedroom gently shakes.

Dawn freshens, the climb is done.
Down towards Glasgow she descends,
Towards the steam tugs, yelping down the glade of cranes
Towards the fields of apparatus, the furnaces
Set on the dark plain like gigantic chessmen.
All Scotland waits for her;
In the dark glens, beside the pale-green sea lochs,
Men long for news.

Letters of thanks, letters from banks,
Letters of joy from the girl and boy,
Receipted bills and invitations
To inspect new stock or visit relations,
And applications for situations,
And timid lovers' declarations,
And gossip, gossip from all the nations,
News circumstantial, news financial,
Letters with holiday snaps to enlarge in,
Letters with faces scrawled on the margin.
Letters from uncles, cousins and aunts,
Letters to Scotland from the South of France,
Letters of condolence to Highlands and Lowlands,
Notes from overseas to the Hebrides;
Written on paper of every hue
The pink, the violet, the white and the blue
The chatty, the catty, the boring, adoring,
The cold and official and the heart's outpouring,
Clever, stupid, short and long,
The typed and the printed and the spelt all wrong.

Thousands are still asleep
Dreaming of terrifying monsters
Or a friendly tea beside the band at Cranston's or Crawford's;
Asleep in working Glasgow, asleep in well-set Edinburgh,
Asleep in granite Aberdeen.
They continue their dreams
But shall wake soon and long for letters.
And none will hear the postman's knock
Without a quickening of the heart,
For who can bear to feel himself forgotten?

W. H. AUDEN

Originally written for the G. P. O.
film NIGHT MAIL

1 Picking up mail: the light string ties break and the bags are carried off their hooks into the van's net.
2 A modern sorting-coach of British Rail.
3 A replica of a Post Office van on the London and Birmingham Railway (1838).
Postal authorities were quick to make use of the railways. In England the Liverpool and Manchester Line began to carry mail in November 1830. In 1838 letter-sorting carriages, automatic pick-up systems and set-down systems all made their appearance. The demands of the Postal authorities were one reason for increased speeds.

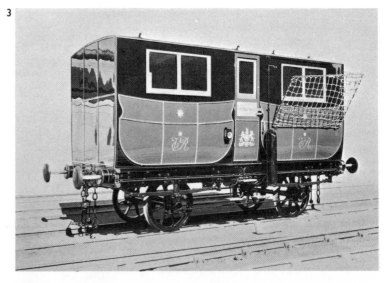

SPEED KINGS

IT IS EXCITING to travel very fast, but breaking records is of less practical importance than are regular sustained fast services. Although the track itself makes the railway the safest means of transport, bends, gradients and other features of the permanent way may regulate the safe speed on a certain stretch. In some places the nature of the terrain will make very high speeds impossible, but where it is possible to level and to straighten out the track the record-breaking locomotives give some indication of what may one day become possible in regular service.

An electrically powered locomotive set the first great record of this century when in 1903 a German locomotive reached the then fantastic speed of 130 m.p.h.

In six decades, this speed has not been equalled by a steam locomotive. It was beaten in 1931 when Germany set up a new record of 143 m.p.h. with the Kruckenburg rail-car. This was an experimental vehicle, driven by a rear-mounted aeroplane propeller. From it were developed the streamlined diesel-electric trains, the *Flying Hamburger* and the *Flying Frankfurter,* which often exceeded 100 m.p.h. and sustained average speeds approaching 80 m.p.h. in regular passenger service: but to reach these speeds the German State Railways had to rebuild most of the track over which the expresses ran.

Streamlining was applied with great success to steam locomotives. In Britain Sir Nigel Gresley built his famous Pacific locomotives. Gresley designed a wedge-shaped front which kept smoke and steam well clear of the driver's cab so that it should not obscure his view. Internal streamlining of the flow of steam, developed by André Chapelon in France, also helped to increase speed.

It was a Gresley locomotive, *the Mallard* A.4 Class Pacific, then No. 4468, which set up an unbeaten record for a steam locomotive

1 The Siemens and Halska electric locomotive which set up a record of 130 m.p.h. in 1903.
2 United States streamliner placed in service in 1942.
3 *The Kruckenburg* rail-car (above) and the *Flying Hamburger* which developed from it.
4 S.N.C.F. locomotive BB. 9004 at the speed trials.
5 United States streamliner *Silver Streak.*
6 205.6 m.p.h.! Electric locomotive CC. 7107.

when on 3rd July 1938, it reached a top speed of 126 m.p.h. It still bears a plaque to commemorate the achievement. The maximum permissible speed on most British main lines is about 90 m.p.h. and the advantages of streamlining at this speed are offset by the difficulties of maintenance when streamlining covers the working parts. For this reason, some British Pacifics have had their streamlining removed until such time as it is possible to operate at increased speeds.

Steam, however, can never hope to catch up with electric traction. On 21st February 1954, CC. 7121, an electric locomotive of French Railways, set up a record of 151 m.p.h. without any special modification. The following year, the S.N.C.F. made preparations for another speed trial, to test the potential of locomotive CC. 7107 of the same class (the type used to haul the *Mistral* express daily between Paris and Lyons at an average speed of 80 m.p.h. and BB. 9004 of a lighter and less powerful class. The transmission system of both locomotives was modified so as to raise the gear ratio to achieve speeds in the neighbourhood of 185 m.p.h.

Preparations for these trials, which included the close inspection of all equipment involved and the making of many special arrangements, lasted nearly a year. To give some idea of what was involved, it was calculated that if 4,000 h.p. was sufficient for a speed of 151 m.p.h., over 10,000 h.p. would be required for 185 m.p.h. To pick up a current of 4,000 amperes at that speed, a special pantograph

had to be designed. Tests were made in a wind tunnel to study the effects of an air current of 185 m.p.h. on the pressure of the pantograph against the traction wire. Locomotives and coaches were fitted with solid monobloc wheels so as to avoid the effects of centrifugal force and of braking on the normal steel-tyred wheel.

All parts which had to rotate at high speeds were tested in workshop pits where they were subjected to rotary speeds equivalent to 280 m.p.h. A two-way radio link was provided between the control post and the driver's cab of each of the locomotives.

The trials took place on the morning of 28th March for the CC. 7107 and on the morning of the 29th the BB. 9004. A speed

of 185 m.p.h. was reached after travelling 13 miles. The two locomotives travelled at over 185 m.p.h. for $7\frac{1}{2}$ miles and at over 199 m.p.h. for nearly 4 miles. The speed of 205.6 m.p.h. was maintained over nearly $1\frac{1}{4}$ miles—a new world record!

The power reached exceeded the estimated figure, and at top speed the locomotives were using 12,000 h.p., which shows the considerable effect of wind resistance at high speeds. Special instruments showed their stability to be very satisfactory.

The United States rail speed record was set by a New York Central Railroad test vehicle, a single passenger coach with two turbo-jet engines mounted on the roof, which reached a speed of 183.85 m.p.h. on 23rd July, 1966.

3

RACK RAILWAYS

IN THE EARLY DAYS of railways many people doubted whether a locomotive with smooth wheels was capable of propelling itself along a smooth track. They thought some more positive grip was required. In 1811 John Blenkinsop patented a system using a pinion on the locomotive which fitted into teeth at the side of the rails, a system which greatly increased the hauling power of the locomotive. In 1812—13 this system was installed on the Middleton, Kenton and Coxlodge Colliery lines. The laying of the Blenkinsop rails and the adoption of steam traction on 12th August 1812 probably made the Leeds-Middleton Colliery line the first steam railway in Britain.

The first American railway locomotive, built by Colonel John Stevens of Hoboken, New Jersey, in 1825, combined a rack-and-pinion system between the rails with guide wheels. The circular demonstration track was America's first steam railway.

In 1831—2 the Neath Abbey Ironworks designed a locomotive combining adhesion and rack operation for Dowlais Ironworks which operated with a rack running parallel to the tramplates.

Thirty years later in America Sylvester Marsh was planning rack railways up the slopes of Mount Washington and Mount Lafayette in New Hampshire. In 1858 he had built a model locomotive and been granted a charter to proceed, and in 1866 he gave a demonstration on a section of track built at his own expense. It was not until a year later, however, that

1 BB. 9233, of the same class as one of the record-holding locomotives, hauling the *Mistral* express in the Valley of the Rhône.
2 New York Central Railroad's jet-powered test car during a run between Butler, Indiana, and Stryker, Ohio.
3 The *Mallard*, which set up an unbeaten record of 126 m.p.h., for a steam locomotive, in 1938.
RACK RAILWAYS
4 The Rigi Railway in 1873.
5 Mount Washington Cog Railway.
6 The Locher system on Mount Pilatus, Switzerland.

sufficient money was raised, and in July 1869 the Mount Washington Cog Railway was carrying passengers to the summit. Today it is very much as when it was built.

In 1863 Nicholas Riggenbach of the Central Swiss Railway patented a system for a rack railway. When he heard of Marsh's system he went to see it in America and found it very like his own.

Back in Europe he and two other engineers (Naeff and Zschokke) obtained a concession to build a rack railway up the 5,905-foot Rigi Mountain. Finally two railways were built, both using his principle, one from the Canton of Lucerne and one from the Canton of Schwyz.

Other railways using the Riggenbach rack were built elsewhere in Switzerland, by Lake Constance from Rorschach to Heiden, up the Kahlenberg near Vienna, up the Corcovado Mountain, Rio de Janiero, and in Angola.

Other systems using racks were devised by a Swiss engineer called Wetli in 1868 and an Italian called Agudio whose rope-worked system was first used on a steep slope on the Turin and Alessandria Railway in 1862.

In 1882 another rack system was patented, by Dr. Roman Abt, consisting of a double pinion running in two stepped tracks arranged so that the teeth of one are opposite the gaps of the other. This system was designed for a line built at Blankenburg in 1884, and has since been used in America, Australia, Japan and India. A line in Colorado, U.S.A., climbs to the summit of Pike's Peak, 14,147 feet above sea level.

The Snowdon Mountain Railway, the only rack railway now operating in Great Britain, works on the Abt principle.

Another system consisting of pairs of pinion wheels mounted horizontally which engage with a flat rack rail with teeth cut in both sides was devised by E. Locher specially for the railway from Alpanachstad up Mount Pilatus in Switzerland, where the gradient is 1 in 3 and sometimes 1 in 2.

5

6

1 & 5 Snowdon Mountain Railway, opened in 1896.
2 The Rigi Railway.
3 A model of John Stevens' locomotive and rail.
4 The new and the old *Old Peppersass* on the Mount
Washington Cog Railway, New Hampshire.
6 A narrow-gauge train on Pike's Peak Railway.

1 Locomotive No. 1008 of the Lancashire and Yorkshire Railway. This 2-4-2 was built in 1889.
2 Great Eastern Railway 0-6-0 locomotive No. 87, built
in 1904 and run on the line to Alexandra Palace.
3 Furness Railway 4-4-0 locomotive No. 3, *Coppernob*,
built in 1846.
4 Great Central Railway 0-4-0 locomotive No. 506,
Butler Henderson, built in 1920.
All these locomotives are now in the Museum of British
Transport, London.

2

3

4

1 A Pullman car of about 1890. A facsimile in the
Museum of British Transport.

TRAVEL IN COMFORT

'DIED FROM EXPOSURE in a second-class carriage of the Great Western Railway' — that was the verdict of an early Victorian inquest on the death of a railway traveller. What happened to the poor devils travelling third or fourth? On this particular line third-class travellers were carried by the night goods trains in ordinary, open wagons with planks laid across to serve as seats and holes bored in the floor to let out the rain. Sometimes passengers simply stood in open boxes.

In 1844 Gladstone, then President of the Board of Trade, pushed the Regulation of Railways Bill through Parliament. It became known as the Cheap Trains Act because, among its provisions, it required that all railway companies should, once a day on each of their lines, provide accommodation for third-class passengers which afforded light, air and protection from the weather at a charge of one penny per mile. These 'cheap trains' were also required to provide a service at an average speed of at least twelve miles per hour.

Some second-class carriages were open with wooden seats; others, 'second-class closed,' were covered boxes with drop windows in the doors—but for anything like comfort it was necessary to travel first-class.

If you owned your own coach you could have it mounted on a truck and travel in that, the horses travelling in a special horse-box. If you travelled in the company's first-class carriages, it was very similar to travelling in a coach. The well-padded seats had head-and elbow-rests and your luggage was out of the way on top. At first, solid padded buffers and linking-chains made every stop and start a very jerky business but, as spring buffers and screw couplings were introduced, the journey became more smooth. For a supplement you could travel in the mail-coach, which seated only two passengers each side, instead of three (or on the broad-gauge Great Western, four).

There were no food facilities on these early trains or toilets (except for some special carriages available for hire by incontinent invalids of ample means), no corridors, no heating (foot-warmers filled with hotwater were provided later) and only oil lamps dropped in through the roof for light. There was, however, a primitive form of sleeper formed by placing two sticks and a cushion across the space between the seats as a sort of stretcher. The sticks could be hired from the guard. Where this was still too short to lie down, a boot was built out beyond the compartment to accommodate the feet. A 'bed-carriage' of this kind was built for Queen Adelaide in 1842.

North American emigrant trains used a similar arrangement, with a board and cushions laid across the seats which could be purchased from the railway staff; but other amenities were available. They had to be, for American trains were unable to go very fast, their track was not designed for speed; distances were considerable and journeys long, so some provision was necessary for passengers to move up and down the train. American carriages soon developed from a simple stage-coach on rails to a long saloon. They were not cut up into separate small compartments but arranged with seats on either side of a central gangway. Stoves for heating, toilets, and mounting on bogies soon became general. Clerestory roofs were used more frequently than in Europe and gave better lighting and ventilation.

Despite these improvements American trains could hardly have been called comfortable. One man, making a night journey in 1853, found conditions so intolerable that he set about devising a comfortable type of sleeping-car. In 1857 George M. Pullman built his first sleeper, a remodelled car called No. 9. It was a primitive affair but, in 1864, after experimenting with sleeping-cars of various designs on the Chicago and Alton Railroad for some years, he produced an elaborate car which he called *The Pioneer*. It cost twenty-thousand dollars and was lavishly fitted—but no one used it. *The Pioneer* was higher and wider than any car then in service on American railroads. It posed clearance problems where station platforms, tunnels and bridges were concerned. But in 1865 it was made part of Abraham Lincoln's funeral train and platforms and bridges from Chicago to Springfield were hurriedly changed to allow for its extra size. From then on *The Pioneer* was a success. In 1867 Pullman joined forces with his competitors, Andrew Carnegie's Central Transportation Company, to form Pullman's Palace Car Company. The same year they produced an 'hotel' car for eating and sleeping and one of these, on the Great Western Railroad of Canada, was the first dining-car.

1—11 (1) Colonial sleeping-car of the Canadian Pacific Railway, 1888. (2) Travel on the Baltimore and Ohio Railroad in 1861. (3) A saloon carriage of the London, Brighton and South Coast Railway, 1873. (4) The kitchen of the Pullman dining-car introduced on the British Great Northern Railway in 1879. (5) European wagon-lit in 1888. (6) Second-class carriage on the Dublin and Kingstown Railway, Ireland, 1837. (7) Early passenger car on the Union Pacific Railway. (8) Wagon-salon in 1889. (9) A train with 'Hotel Sleeping Cars,' 1875. (10) Wagon-lit in 1877. (11) Great Western Railway third-class carriage, *circa* 1855.

In 1874 the Midland Railway in England imported Pullman cars from America. Mounted on four-wheeled bogies, these long-bodied carriages had central passageways, lavatories, hot-water radiators running from a stove and kerosene lamps for illumination. Day travel was in drawing-room cars with a row of pivoted armchairs on each side of the gangway. Sleeping accommodation was in two-tier curtained berths. The upper berths folded up to the roof and the lower ones turned into two comfortable seats for day-time use.

In 1879 a Pullman car running between London and Leeds on the Great Northern Railway provided the first regular dining service on a British train, with the meals cooked on board.

On 4th December 1876, two years after the first Pullman in Great Britain, a Belgian engineer, Georges Nagelmackers, founded the Compagnie Internationale des Wagons-Lits. Reassured by the success of Pullman in America, Nagelmackers sought to provide 'vehicles which would carry travellers making long journeys with the maximum of comfort, notably by making it possible to have complete rest in real beds put at their disposal for the night.' The complexity of European rail systems and the difficulties encountered with Customs and Police at every frontier made innumerable changes of train necessary. The company was planned on an international basis, outside the various railway administrations, and aimed to provide comfortable through-coaches in which passengers could travel throughout their journey without having to change trains.

By the beginning of 1877 contracts had been signed with twenty-one different railway companies for wagons-lits. To the wagons-lits were added wagons-restaurants and, despite the obstacles presented by the lack of standardisation, either of equipment or regulations, the first great international express ran in 1883: the *Orient Express*.

In May 1883 the C.I.W.L. signed agreements with the different companies over whose lines the *Orient Express* would have to pass.

The first train ran on 5th June. The journey from Paris to Constantinople (Istanbul) took eighty-one hours and thirty minutes. Following a route north of the Alps (the Simplon Tunnel was not opened until 1906), passengers travelled direct to Vienna, Budapest and Bucharest but at Giurgeva, a little port on the Danube, they crossed from the Rumanian to the Bulgarian bank in a ferry-steamer and then boarded another train for a seven-hour journey to Varna, on the Black Sea. There they took a packet of the Lloyd-Austria Line and after another fifteen hours docked in Constantinople.

Meanwhile, in Britain, native-built coaches were becoming more comfortable. In January 1875 the Midland Railway, followed later by the other companies, abolished the second class and began to build its third class with upholstered seats. Coaches were mounted on four- or six-wheel bogies; clerestory roofs were built and, to improve illumination, coal gas, oil gas and, in 1881, electricity were used. The year 1881 also saw, on the Great Northern Railway, the first ordinary British train to have a corridor. It led only to the toilet, there was no connection with the adjoining coach. Eight years later the Midland Railway had gone so far as to install lavatories in its third class, and by 1891 the Great Western Railway had built a through-corridor train.

One interesting feature of British railways in the latter half of the nineteenth century was the family saloon—consisting of a main saloon furnished with armchairs, a table and sofa seats, smaller compartments, including perhaps a smoking-room, a second-class compartment for servants, baggage room, toilet, and sometimes a kitchen. These carriages were made available to parties who made a block booking above a certain number of tickets. The railway companies would undertake to take one to any destination without disturbance to the occupants, providing the sort of direct service which Nagelmackers sought to give to travellers on the Continent.

1 and 2 A three-tier compartment in a modern sleeping-car which converts from (1) to (2) for day use.
3 Restaurant car in 1908, interior.
4 Restaurant car in 1906, exterior.
5 A single compartment in a modern sleeping-car.
6 A modern wagon-lit.

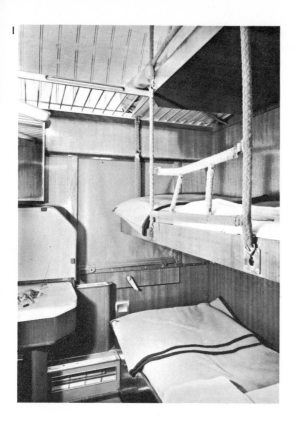

EMIGRANT'S BED

I SUPPOSE the reader has some notion of an American railroad-car, that long narrow wooden box, like a flat-roofed Noah's ark, with a stove and a convenience, one at either end, a passage down the middle, and transverse benches upon either hand. Those destined for emigrants on the Union Pacific are only remarkable for their extreme plainness, nothing but wood entering in any part into their constitution, and for the usual inefficacy of the lamps, which often went out and shed but a dying glimmer even while they burned. The benches are too short for anything but a young child. Where there is scarce elbow-room for two to sit, there will not be space enough for one to lie. Hence the Company, or rather, as it appears from certain bills about the Transfer Station, the Company's servants, have conceived a plan for the better accommodation of travellers. They prevail on every two to chum together. To each of the chums they sell a board and three square cushions stuffed with straw, and covered with thin cotton. The benches can be made to face each other in pairs, for the backs are reversible. On the approach of night the boards are laid from bench to bench, making a couch wide enough for two, and long enough for a man of the middle height; and the chums lie down side by side upon the cushions with the head to the conductor's van and the feet to the engine. When the train is full, of course this plan is impossible, for there must not be more than one to every bench, neither can it be carried out unless the chums agree. It was to bring about this last condition that our white-haired official now bestirred himself. He made a most active master of ceremonies, introducing likely couples, and even guaranteeing the amiability and honesty of each. The greater the number of happy couples the better for his pocket, for it was he who sold the raw material of the beds. His price for one board and three straw cushions began with two dollars and a half; but before the train left, and, I am sorry to say, long after I had purchased mine, it had fallen to one dollar and a half.

FROM 'ACROSS THE PLAINS'
BY ROBERT LOUIS STEVENSON

---

1 A carriage used for emigrants, 1883.
2 Interior of an emigrant carriage, 1884.
3—6 Fast and comfortable diesel Pullman trains are bringing back passengers to British Rail services. Operating on several different routes, they offer air-conditioning, adjustable seats and fine food.

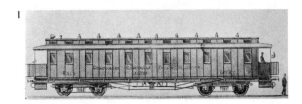

LUXURY TODAY

AS THE YEARS have passed passenger accommodation has improved for all classes, but recent years have seen particular efforts by the railways to compete with other forms of transport by providing extra comforts and services.

Long-distance routes, such as American transcontinental expresses which take two days to complete the journey, have upheld the tradition of Pullman's Palace Cars and counter the attraction of airliner speeds with a level of comfort and luxury impossible in the air. Restaurants, lounges, bars, domed compartments for better sightseeing, and a much greater variety of sleeper accommodation than the European first and second class and couchette make the trip a pleasant holiday for the traveller who does not demand the speed of jet aeroplanes.

One of these luxury trains, the Great Northern Railway's *Empire Builder,* which takes 43 hours 50 minutes to complete the 2,210 miles from Chicago to Seattle, cost £$1\frac{1}{4}$ million to equip and has a staff of 25, not counting the locomotive crew, to look after only 323 passengers.

Services directed at the businessman have been another field, particularly in Europe, where the railways have been at pains to attract and increase custom. In 1954 the railway authorities of Belgium, France, West Germany, Italy, Luxembourg, the Netherlands and Switzerland planned a new service of comfortable, high-speed trains linking 90 of the major cities and industrial centres of Western Europe. These *Trans-Europ-Expresses* are scheduled to suit the businessman's convenience, with

timings that compare favourably with those
for road transport or for air travel plus in and
out of city times. They have proved a great
success. The same principle is now being
applied to freight with *Trans-Europ-Express
Marchandises* which operates fast scheduled
freight services between eighteen countries,
aided by simplified Customs procedures.

Facilities for the traveller today do not stop
at providing excellent restaurant and sleeping
accommodation. Secretarial services, radio, re-
layed music, radio telephones, film shows—all
these can be found on wheels, and so long
as the present competition for the traveller's
custom continues no doubt more services will
become available.

6

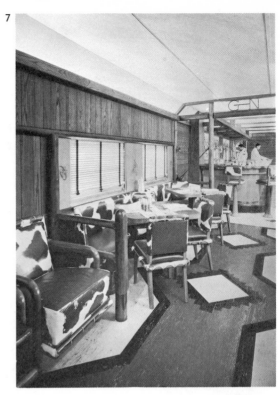

7

8

1—7 The Great Northern Railway of America's transcontinental streamliner which departs daily from Chicago for Seattle and Portland, provides three domed sections, and a full-length domed lounge for sight-seeing (which provide spectacular views of the Montana Rockies. Dining-cars and lounges are decorated with Indian and ranch motifs.

8—10 The Santa Fé Railroad's express running between Chicago and Los Angeles has comfortable reclining seats set four feet above the rails giving a smoother ride with less noise and vibration. There is a sightseeing 'pleasure dome' and a special feature is the Turquoise Room (9), one of the first private dining-rooms on any railroad.

9

10

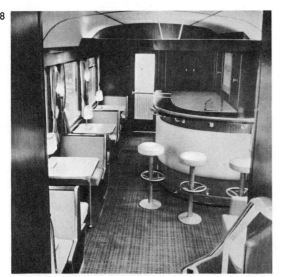

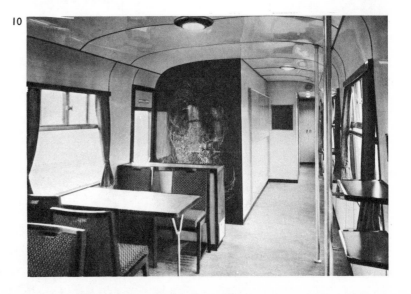

1 The Italian State Railways' *Settebello* has a forward observation car; the driver's cab is mounted above the observation department.
2, 3, 8, 9. The West German *Rheingold* express features provision for secretaries (3), a comfortable bar and an observation car.
4 A panoramic car of the French Railways.
5 The bar in a diesel train-set on Cuba's rail system.
6 Radio-telephones are now available on some French routes.
7 A dining-car on the *Canadian Pacific Express*.
10 A buffet-car on British Rail's diesel 'Trans-Pennine' service.

1, 2 Observation cars are not a new idea, this one was photographed in service on the Llandudno—Llanberis line in Wales in 1912, but modern observation domes like that of the *Canadian* (2) give an even better view.

3—7 *Trans-Europ-Express* service of (3) Swiss Railways, (4) Italian State Railways, (5) German State Railways, (6) French Railways. The Swiss electric train seen here on the shores of Lake Geneva is able to run on any of four different line currents. All the other train-sets are diesel powered. Trans-Europe inter-city routes are shown in (7). The building of a Channel Tunnel will make it possible to extend the TEE and TEEM services to major British cities. Although some difficulties will be encountered because British routes were built for smaller rolling stock and often do not give sufficient clearance for continental vehicles, and the slight difference in gauge is critical at high speeds, ways will be found of overcoming these difficulties.

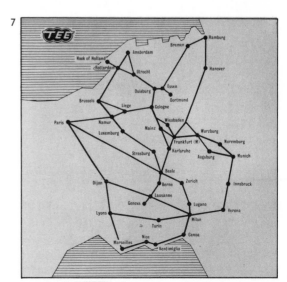

TO A LOCOMOTIVE IN WINTER

THEE for my recitative,
Thee in the driving storm even as now, the snow, the winter-day
    declining,
Thee in thy panoply, thy measur'd dual throbbing and thy beat
    convulsive,
Thy black cylindric body, golden brass and silvery steel,
Thy ponderous side-bars, parallel and connecting rods, gyrating,
    shuttling at thy sides,
Thy matrical, now swelling pant and roar, now tapering in the
    distance,
Thy great protruding head-light fix'd in front,
Thy long, pale, floating vapor-pennants, tinged with delicate
    purple,
The dense and murky clouds out-belching from thy smoke-
    stack,
Thy knitted frame, thy springs and valves, the tremulous twinkle
    of thy wheels,
Thy train of cars behind, obedient, merrily following,
Through gale or calm, now swift, now slack, yet steadily
    careering;
Type of the modern—emblem of motion and power—pulse of
    the continent,
For once come serve the Muse and merge in verse, even as here
    I see thee,
With storm and buffeting gusts of wind and falling snow,
By day thy warning ringing bell to sound its notes,
By night thy silent signal lamps to swing.

Fierce-throated beauty!
Roll through my chant with all thy lawless music, thy swinging
    lamps at night,
Thy madly-whistled laughter, echoing, rumbling like an earth-
    quake, rousing all,
Law of thyself complete, thine own track firmly holding,
(No sweetness debonair of tearful harp or glib piano thine,)
Thy trills of shrieks by rocks and hills return'd,
Launch'd o'er the prairies wide, across the lakes,
To the free skies unpent and glad and strong.

WALT WHITMAN

NARROW-GAUGE RAILWAYS

TO MOST PEOPLE in Europe and America the 'standard' gauge for railways today is 4 ft. $8\frac{1}{2}$ in. and they consider anything less as 'narrow gauge,' but in some countries (the U.S.S.R., India, Brazil, Spain, Ireland and Australia, for instance, who have a wider gauge) 4 ft. $8\frac{1}{2}$ in. would be considered narrow. Indeed, many early American and British railways were built to wider gauges than today. Isambard Kingdom Brunel, the great engineer, built his Great Western line to a 7-foot gauge. When a standardised gauge became imperative in Britain, pressure from the 4 ft. $8\frac{1}{2}$ in. lines caused Parliament to declare for the present standard and Brunel's line first had a narrow track laid between its metals, and then was taken up altogether. The last Great Western wide-gauge locomotive ran in 1892.

Wide gauge gives greater stability because a lower centre of gravity is possible in the rolling-stock, but it requires more solid support, wider bridges and smoother bends—all of which can add enormously to the cost of line construction. Some people think that the demands of modern heavy, high-speed traffic will lead to the adoption of a broader gauge.

A narrow gauge can also have great advantages, provided that very high speeds are not required. A narrow gauge can take sharp bends and follow natural gradients much more easily, so that the engineering difficulties and expenses of construction are reduced, and the rolling-stock is lighter, and therefore cheaper. These advantages led to the adoption of narrow-gauge track for mine and quarry railways and other industrial closed systems, for railways in very difficult terrain, and for small local lines even in countries where a larger gauge was standard. In other countries a narrow gauge was adopted as the usual size.

Those railways which are narrower than their country's standard gauge are usually either used for industrial purposes or have become pleasure lines. Many of the local pas-

---

1 A would-be engine driver on the Ravenglass and Eskdale Railway, Cumberland.
2 The last broad-gauge train in Britain, seen in Sonning Cutting.
3 The Hoot, Toot and Whistle Railway, near Chicago.

senger lines have been forced to close by the competition of road transport. Those that remain do so because they are the only means of reaching a particular beauty spot or because they have sufficient interest in themselves to attract passengers 'just for the ride'.

The miniature and the oddity are always fascinating and many narrow-gauge lines have both, for their locomotives and rolling-stock are far from standard patterns. In many places miniature lines have been specially built as an attraction in themselves and these are frequently operated by locomotives and stock which are scaled-down replicas of standard equipment. Some lines have rolling-stock which reproduces historic locomotives and carriages—the Hoot, Toot and Whistle Railway, for instance, has everything in the style of 1860 and a miniature version of the famous locomotive *The General*.

In the U.S.S.R., Czechoslovakia and Hun-gary there are a number of narrow-gauge railways which are run by boys and girls. Here there is an opportunity for every boy to satisfy his ambition to be an engine driver and they play a valuable part in training young people for railway work.

1 *Talyllyn* Locomotive No. 1, pulls a train into Dolgoch station on the Talyllyn line, originally a quarry railway.
2 The 2 ft. gauge Darjeeling Railway in the Himalayas. The men on the front of the locomotive drop sand on the rails to stop slipping.
3 A young engine driver on the Young Pioneers' Railway at Kharkov in the Ukraine.
4 French Railways' 1300 h.p. Z. 7100 rail-car, in use on the electrified line between Lyons and Saint-Etienne. Its maximum speed is 74 m.p.h. It can seat 70 passengers and haul three trailers.
5 An electric train entering Castellamare di Stabia Station on the narrow-gauge Circum-Vesuviana Railway between Naples and Sorrento.

4

5

ROYAL AND STATE TRAINS

AT TWENTY-FIVE PAST TWELVE on 11th June 1842 a young woman of twenty-three stepped down from a carriage at Paddington Station to join her husband on the platform. Railway travel had become respectable. Queen Victoria had made her first train journey.

Two years before, the Great Western Railway 'anticipating the Patronage of the Queen and her illustrious Consort, Prince Albert, and of the members of the Royal Family,' had ordered a 'splendid railway carriage' from the famous London coach-builder David Davies.

'It is a very handsome vehicle 21 feet in length and divided into three compartments, the two end ones being four feet six inches long and nine feet wide, while the centre forms a noble saloon, twelve feet long, nine feet wide and six feet six inches high. The exterior is painted of the same brown colour as the others of the Company's carriages, and at each end is a large window affording a view of the whole of the line. The interior has been most magnificently fitted up by Mr. Webb, upholsterer, Old Bond Street. The saloon is handsomely decorated with hanging sofas in the rich style of Louis XIV, and the walls are panelled out in the same elegant manner, and fitted up with rich crimson and white silk and exquisitely executed paintings representing the four elements by Parris. The end compartments are also fitted up in the same style, each apartment having in the centre a useful and ornamental rose-wood table; and the floors of the whole are covered with chequered India matting.'

Originally designed to run on four wheels, it was modified to run on eight—perhaps at the suggestion of Prince Albert or Queen Adelaide, who were already railway travellers.

When the railway company received unexpected instructions that the Queen wished to be conveyed by rail from Slough to London, they assembled a train for the royal party

The Royal Railroad Carriage.

drawn by *Phlegethon*, an almost new locomotive with seven-foot driving wheels.

The Queen drove by coach from Windsor Castle and while the royal coaches were being loaded on to flat cars she inspected the line. The locomotive was driven by Daniel Gooch, its designer, who was Locomotive Superintendent of the line, accompanied by Brunel, the company's Engineer.

The Queen enjoyed her first rail journey and wrote to her uncle, the King of the Belgians: 'We arrived here yesterday morning having come by railroad, from Windsor, in half an hour, free from dust and crowd and heat, and I am quite charmed by it.'

1 Queen Victoria's saloon, built by the London and North Western Railway in 1869, now in the Museum of British Transport.
2 The Queen's saloon carriage designed by Richard Mansell for the South Eastern Railway and built in 1851.
3 A coloured print of the Queen's carriage which opened to show the Royal Family inside.

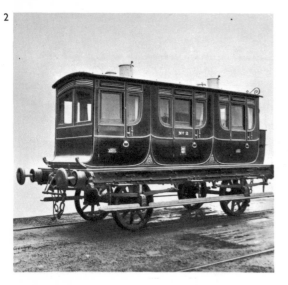

1 The Royal Saloon built at Wolverton Works in 1941 and still used by Elizabeth II.
2 Queen Adelaide's coach, built by the London and Birmingham Railway in 1842.
3 The sleeping arrangements in Queen Adelaide's coach. Note the padded stretcher between the seats and the 'boot' to accommodate the royal feet.
4 Twin saloons built for Queen Victoria in 1869 were joined on a single frame to form this carriage in 1895.
5 The carriage used by Oscar II of Sweden for official trips.
6 The bedroom in Queen Alexandra's 1903 saloon.
7 A locomotive decorated for a royal tour of Cardiff Docks in 1907.
8 The papal train of Pope Pius IX.

United States Car No. 1: the Official Carriage of the President.
1 The Lounge.
2 The Dining Room.
3 Exterior.

RAILWAYS AND THE COUNTRYSIDE

TOO OFTEN the railways have been associated with grimy buildings and dirty back-to-back houses huddled beneath embankments. These things exist, it is true; however, they are not caused by the railway but by the sudden development of industry which railways made possible, and the urbanisation which followed. Indeed, in the early days, when locomotives burned coke, not coal, there was no dirty smoke, nor will there be in the future when our railways are diesel- or electric-powered. Another charge which has been brought is that they have defaced the countryside. Wordsworth was among the people who decried the railways; an angry Ruskin said, 'I detest railways. Your railway has cut through some of the loveliest bits of scenery in the country,' and many landowners opposed them, though more, perhaps, for fear of damage to their hunting than fear of damage to the natural scene.

However, after a century which had seen the drastic change following the increasing enclosure of the land, the building of turnpike roads and of canals cutting across the countryside, many people thought of the new cuttings and embankments not as scars but as arteries carrying life to the countryside.

The author of *Osborne's London and Birmingham Railway Guide* describes that railway as '. . . a piece of human workmanship of the most stupendous kind; which, when considered with respect to its scientific character, magnitude, utility, its harmony of arrangement, and mechanical contrivance, eclipses all former works of art. Compared to it, how shabby a structure would be the celebrated Roman Wall, or even the more extensive one of the Chinese; as for the Egyptian pyramids, they so far from being fit to be mentioned in comparison with the railway, are merely uncouth monuments . . .' A guide book to Surrey, describing the view from the North Downs in 1865, says: 'The railway lines from Redhill to Dorking, from East Grinstead to Three Bridges and from Redhill far on the way to Brighton, are visible from this point; the wreaths of white smoke that float above the deep foliage of the Weald marking the progress of the trains across the old country of the Iguanodon and the Plesiosaurus.'

George Eliot, too, seems to have found pleasure in the sight of the railways:

'Our Midland plains have never lost their familiar impression and conservative spirit for me; yet at every other mile, since I first looked on them some sign of world-wide change some new direction of human labour, has wrought itself into what one may call the speech of the landscape . . . While hardly a wrinkle is made in the fading mother's face, or a new curve of health in the blooming girl's, the hills are cut through, or the breaches between them spanned, we choose our level, and the white steam-pennon flies along it.'

1 The Avon Viaduct, Wolston, Warwickshire. From a drawing by John Bourne.
2 A cutting near Roade, Northamptonshire.

THE ARCHITECTURE OF THE RAILWAYS

THE RAILWAYS cut across the countryside, but the taste and skill of the great railway architects and engineers ensured that they contributed to the shape of the countryside. Change was unavoidable, but as much was gained as lost. Pioneers like George and Robert Stephenson and Isambard Kingdom Brunel, building without the use of steel, designed so well that their bridges and viaducts can still be used today, and for much heavier traffic than they were ever intended to carry. Their earthworks, cuttings and embankments were among their greatest achievements, although perhaps least noticed by the traveller today.

Aware of the magnitude of their task they decorated their tunnel entrances with fine arches, some grandly classical, others more fanciful with gothick crenellations or exotic shapes. Set at the end of stark cuttings (since softened by a century's vegetation), they must have been even more imposing than they are today.

At first Robert Stephenson thought that locomotives should not be expected to haul on gradients steeper than 1 in 330, so viaducts were built to carry the line at an even level. These viaducts, and the many bridges to carry the line over waterways and roads, were often a graceful addition to the scene and bear comparison with the fine aqueducts of Imperial Rome.

But such features had been seen before. One thing the railway demanded for which no other form of transport had shown a need — a proper station building. The stage-coach had used a convenient inn as a departure point or relay station where its passengers could shelter, but the railway had to have a building on its tracks. The requirements were a place where passengers could buy their tickets and await the departure of the train and have easy access to the carriages themselves.

Mount Clare, the first station in the United States, provided little more than a booking office with no other shelter for the passenger; but the first British station, at Crown Street, Liverpool, embodied many features of the modern station. There was a vehicle court, separated from street traffic by a wall, a combined ticket-selling and waiting room and both covered access to the carriages and a train-shed right across the tracks.

Many variations in station buildings were

1 The entrance to Bristol Long Tunnel at Foxes' Wood.
2 The entrance to Box Tunnel.
3 Isambard Kingdom Brunel, the great rival of the Stephensons; among his achievements were the Royal Albert Bridge at Saltash, the steam ship *Great Eastern*— and the Great Western broad-gauge line.
4 The Conway Bridge was dressed up to match the castle by order of Act of Parliament.
5 The Britannia Tubular Bridge across the Menai Straits, built by Robert Stephenson.
6 Wharncliffe Viaduct, a drawing by J. C. Bourne.
7 The viaduct across the Rhine at Eglisau.

tried. The first, of which Crown Street was an example, had a single platform on one side of the tracks only. Next came two facing platforms for arriving and departing passengers, as at the first Euston Station (1835—9) with waiting, baggage and booking facilities on the departure side. The great drawback of this type was that when the volume of traffic became too great to be handled by one platform at each side, intermediate platforms had to be added. To reach them, cross-platforms or foot-bridges were necessary. At Paddington, where there was no space for a cross-platform, Brunel installed a sort of drawbridge which could be withdrawn and stored under the platforms when not in use. Naturally, while in position these got in the way of the trains, but passengers preferred them to using footbridges.

Another plan was that of the head-type station with the offices in a building at the head of the tracks and platforms perpendicular to it—a scheme particularly suited to terminal stations but equally suited for use where the tracks can be made to pass below the station building.

The European railway companies and their architects sought to make their stations, and particularly the terminals, a symbol of the importance of their enterprise. The grand scale of Euston, with its imposing Doric 'propylaeum' forming, as it were, a gateway to the railways of England, made a great impression on the departing traveller, and many stations boasted a classically styled portico.

In some towns the architect tried to harmonise his building with the aspect and the spirit of the town itself. It is interesting to note that Brunel took the medieval abbey at Bath as the model for his station there, not the 'classical' architecture of the Georgian town.

Not every station was built on imposing lines. Small stations, sometimes built of local stone, fitted comfortably into the countryside. Frequently seeking to emulate a domestic style, they suggested a chalet or *cottage orné*. An Italianate style became very popular; in smaller stations looking like villas and in larger ones, to which a campanile was often added, suggesting an Italian palace. The *Illustrated London News* in 1844 stated that the South East Railway Company had selected the 'Italian Palazzo style' for its buildings: 'the choice having been determined by the convenience

of its general arrangement, its cheapness and the suitability of its picturesque decorations to the bustling character of a railway site . . . the campanile made here to serve the useful purpose of a clock tower—is certainly a striking and appropriate feature.'

In the New World the station buildings took second place. The capital was all needed for the building of the line itself. Many stations consisted of only a single room, and until the building of the Old Grand Central Station in New York in 1869, there was nothing in America to compare with the great European stations.

Not everyone agreed that railway stations

should be either monumental or highly decorated. While people flocked to see Hardwick's Euston arch, Pugin thought: 'The architects have evidently considered it an opportunity for *showing off what they could do* instead of *carrying out what required*. Hence the colossal Grecian portico or gateway, 100 feet high [an exaggeration—the overall height was only 72 feet] for the cabs to drive through, and set down a few feet further at the 14-inch brick wall and sash window booking office. This piece of Brobdignaggian absurdity must have cost the company a sum which would have built a first-rate station replete with convenience and which would have been really grand

from its simplicity.'

William Cubitt said: 'A good station could be built at King's Cross for less than the cost of the ornamental archway at Euston Square.'

Considering some of Pugin's own highly gothic designs, it is a little difficult to understand his wish for simplicity. King's Cross, however, was built in 1851—2 by Cubitt's brother in an effectively simple style at a cost of £123,000 (the Euston arch cost £35,000).

The first station at Liverpool embodied the idea of a roof covering all the tracks, a concept more often rejected now in favour of separate platform covers. This idea of the 'train-shed' gave the architects an opportunity to join a competition which has been going on since the first arch was built—to construct the widest possible unsupported span.

Crown Street had a modest wooden shed 30 feet wide, but within a few years sheds were being supported on iron columns and then, when it was seen how quickly wood deteriorated from the smoke and steam of the locomotives, were made entirely of iron.

In 1854 a single span of 211 feet at New Street Station, Birmingham, exceeded the span of the dome of St. Peter's Basilica in Rome and every other earlier vault.

The great arched roof was by no means the only form of train-shed, but it was the most spectacular. At St. Pancras, London, a span of 243 feet was built in 1863—76, not to be exceeded until 1888 when the Pennsylvania

1 Mount Clare Station of the Baltimore and Ohio Railroad, America's first railway station.
2 Crown Street, Liverpool, a print by Bury, dated 1831. Note the turntables for reversing locomotives and rolling-stock, and the cable working of the centre track.
3 Paddington Station, which replaced the Bishop's Road terminus of Brunel's Great Western Railway. The original roof arches still stand.
4 The First Thüringer Banhof, Leipzig (1840-4), architect Eduard Pötsch. The tracks meet at a turntable in front of the forecourt.
5 London Bridge Station, terminus of the Brighton, Dover and Croydon Railway (1844).
6 The village station at East Farleigh, Kent.
7 The 'new station house' at Washington, D.C., built in 1852.
8 The Euston 'propylaeum' designed by Philip Hardwick was built of Yorkshire stone and cost £35,000. It has been demolished to make way for a new Euston.
9 Cubitt's station at King's Cross.
10 New Street Station, Birmingham, about 1905.

1

2

3

4

5

6

7

8

Railroad's station at Jersey City was built with a span of 252 feet. The climax was reached with 300 feet at the second Broad Street Station, Philadelphia, in 1892—30.

Not only did the train-shed grow larger as the traffic and the number of platforms increased, the head-block also became larger and more complex. Sometimes fronted by an imposing façade, sometimes sheltering behind a great hotel, as at Paddington or St. Pancras, there had to be provision for additional passenger services, offices for company staff and often the opportunity was taken to add grandeur for its own sake.

Euston was once more in the lead when Philip Charles Hardwick, son of the original architect, added the richly decorated 'Great Hall' which was soon copied by other designers.

The head-buildings began to incorporate shops, restaurants, barbers' shops, bathrooms, in later years even cinemas, as well as the necessary booking, waiting, baggage and toilet facilities for the passenger. Instead of proceeding directly via the ticket office to the platform, with a waiting-room near by if he was early for his train, the passenger had to find his way through an assemblage of halls, corridors, concourses, arcades and staircases. The simpler utilitarian functions of the station were hidden under vast masonry designed chiefly to impress. In North America particularly many opulent buildings were erected, some of them railway cities where all the requirements of life could be found without ever leaving the station building.

One American station which uses a colossal scale without loss of functional efficiency is the Grand Central Station in New York, built 1903—13. However, highly satisfactory though the planning of this station is, the cost of operating it is proving uneconomic today.

The great glass-arch train-shed was going out of favour in the United States by 1914. Ten years before, Lincoln Bush had patented his form of shedding of low-reinforced concrete spans with slots to allow fumes and smoke to escape. This style in turn was supplanted by the simple platform canopy making no attempt to cover the lines or provide protection from stormy weather.

Train-sheds continued to be built in Europe. In 1930 the new Stazione Centrale at Milan

1 The second Broad Street Station, Philadelphia.
2 The train-shed of St. Pancras.
3 Stazione Santa Maria Novella, Florence.
4 The front of St. Pancras, originally designed as a great hotel.
5 Ohio Union Terminal, Cincinnati.
6 The Great Hall at Euston (now demolished).
7 The main concourse, Grand Central Terminal, New York City.
8 Roma Termini in 1869.
9 Roma Termini in 1874.
10 and 11. The magnificent modern Roma Termini has platforms running directly from a wide internal piazza which stretches the full width of the building, forming a thoroughfare with shops and restaurants. The dramatic curve of the roof echoes the line of the remains of the wall of Septimius Serverus, seen at the end of the booking hall (11).

1 Naples (1839).
2 Lime Street, Liverpool (1836).
3 Derby (1839), architect Francis Thompson. Note the graceful fluted columns with their ribbon motif.
4 & 6 Pennsylvania Station, New York City: façade and main concourse.
5 Union Terminal, Washington, D.C.
7 New station at Plymouth, Devon.
8 Stairs and bridges at Coventry, Warwickshire (1962).
9 Bochum, West Germany (1956).
10 Cologne, main station.
11 Johannesburg, South Africa.
12 Napoli Centrale.
13 Concourse of Montreal Central.
14 Kuala Lumpur, Malaya.
15 S. Lucia, Venice. The steps of this new station lead straight down to the Grand Canal.

1 S. Maria Novella, Florence, arrival platform (1848).
2 The new Napoli Centrale station features this vigorous roof treatment.

MORE BRIDGES

3 Forth Bridge, Scotland. Each of the centre spans is 1,710 feet long.
4 Kaaimans River Bridge, Cape Province, South Africa.
5 & 7. Niagara Falls, 1861 and 1897.
6 Joise River Bridge, South Africa.

was completed. Built from designs by Ulisse Stacchini which won a competition in 1913 it has a beautiful series of five simple arched spans, the largest of which is 236 feet wide. Unfortunately, this simplicity is not carried through to the head-building, which is probably

the most pompous and grandiose of its kind. Compare it with the stark simplicity of the Stazione Santa Maria Novella designed by G. Michelucci and finished only six years later. Here the function and direction of the platforms and tracks are expressed in the lines of the head-building and the glassed panel of the porte-cochère.

Scandinavia, Holland, Germany, Austria and Great Britain have all produced good station designs in recent years but, to my mind, the most satisfying station in the world today is again in Italy—the fine Stazione Termini in Rome.

This, perhaps, is the type of station we shall see in the future.

1 Royal Albert Bridge across the River Tamar at Saltash, Cornwall, built by Brunel and opened in 1859.
2 La Voulte Viaduct across the Rhône in France, is the longest railway structure in pre-stressed concrete.
3 Hurricane Gulch Bridge, Alaska.
4 Fades Viaduct, France, the highest in the world.
5 Grandfey Viaduct, Switzerland.
6 The Landwasser Viaduct on the Rhaetian Railway's main line from Chur to St. Moritz, Switzerland.

LONDON TO BIRMINGHAM IN 1838

TICKET IN HAND we pass through to the departure platform and find our numbered seats. We have a five and a half hour journey ahead of us in an open second-class carriage, single fare twenty shillings. If we paid more we could travel in one of the six-seater, closed-in first-class carriages or even in one of the four-seater mail carriages, but second-class *closed* carriages only run at night.

The officials are already shouting for us to take our places and as soon as we are settled some of the railway staff push the train of carriages to the end of the departure platform where they are attached to a continuous cable by which we are hauled up to Chalk Farm by a powerful winding engine. There the locomotive, one of Edward Bury's little engines with a tall chimney and shining brass dome, is attached.

AUSTRALIAN RAILWAYS
1 Two '44' class diesel-electric locomotives.
2 An inter-urban electric train leaving Sydney Station.
3 A '46' class electric locomotive in the Blue Mountain region of New South Wales.
LONDON AND BIRMINGHAM RAILWAY
4 Philip Hardwick's great Doric arch was the gateway to the London and Birmingham Railway. Passengers entering through it were set down under a colonnaded covered way. First-class passengers entered through the north door, bought their tickets at the booking office and then went down a corridor to their waiting-room. Second-class passengers used another door to a combined waiting-room and booking office. Hand baggage was carried to the waiting-room and heavy trunks and cases loaded on to the train from a baggage dock at the end of the lines.
To the right of the 'propylaeum' a gate led to the carriage dock. The nobility and gentry could arrive in their own carriages, which were then placed on flat wagons, the horses travelling in a special horse-box. The passenger could either travel in his own carriage or in the company's. When he reached the end of his journey the carriage was taken down, the horses harnessed, and milord could drive off straight away.
5 The departure platform, Euston.
6 The fixed engine station at Camden Town. To cross the Regent's Canal, near Chalk Farm, the line had to be given a gradient of 1 in 70. This section, known as the Camden Inclined Plane, was thought too steep for locomotive operation and until 1844 was worked by cable. The trains were attached to an endless rope, 4,080 yards long and $2\frac{1}{4}$ inches thick, which was operated by two 60 h.p. engines at the top of the incline. Men known as 'bankriders' travelled on incoming trains to manipulate the brakes and prevent the speed exceeding 10 m.p.h.

With a jerk we are really on our way. 'The noise made by the engine is at first somewhat between a pant and a cough; but this becomes less distinct as our rapidity increases, for the motion of the piston which occasions the coughing sound, when it becomes rapid, connects the sound into a continuous burring noise ... by no means so unpleasant as the noise of the stage coach.'

We are approaching the Primrose Hill Tunnel, 1,154 yards long, so we put on our gauze spectacles to protect our eyes against the soot and smoke—anyone without spectacles should keep their eyes closed when passing through tunnels. A railway constable at the lineside shows a white flag to indicate that the line is clear and into the darkness we go. A rain of sparks bounces back off the roof but we are soon out in the air again, passing the villages of Hampstead and Highgate away on the right, and on through Kilburn.

By now we must be rushing at a speed of at least twenty miles an hour and we roar through Kensal Green Tunnel in no time at all, past the place where Willesden Junction, one of the largest railway centres in the country, will appear in later years; but now the open fields and farmsteads give no sign that they are so soon to be swallowed up by the spread of London's houses and factories.

The train rushes on, up the long gradient to Hatch End with the buildings of Harrow School away on the crest of Harrow Hill to the left, and then down through Bushey and over a magnificent viaduct into Watford. Here, whilst the train makes its first stop and takes water to refill the thirsty boiler, we may admire the neat 'Gothic building, the residence of the inspector of the station.'

Soon we are jolting into motion again and entering Watford Tunnel, 1,817 yards long, with five ventilation shafts. We can feel quite safe for 'great attention is paid by the policemen to detect any obstruction on the rails in the tunnel.' From the tunnel we reach the lower slopes of the Chilterns and pound through Boxmoor (the original terminus when the first section of the line was opened last year). The calm waters of the Grand Junction Canal run alongside us until we top the rise at Tring and roll downhill into the great Tring Cutting, its white chalk walls agleam in the September sunshine.

The Stephensons, father and son, can be proud of this achievement. Two and a half miles long, in places sixty feet deep, it took 400 men three and a half years to make, excavating one and three-quarter million tons of soil Another few miles, then through the tunnel at Leighton and on to Denbigh Hall where, since April until only the other day, passengers had to transfer to a horse-coach for the trip to Rugby; but now the Kilsby Tunnel is all complete and we go straight through.

Our next stop is at Wolverton and here, fifty-two and a half miles from London, the engines are changed. 'The trains stop at this station 10 minutes, and a female attendant has been placed here for the convenience of ladies.' Here too are workshops, artisans, etc., and every convenience, to repair accidents, or to obtain any requisite which the trains may require.'

Seven miles further on we reach Roade, from which horse-coaches connect with Northampton (fare 1s 6d), then on to Blisworth through a great cutting which, though not the largest on the line, was the most difficult and expensive. The ground consists largely of hard blue limestone and this had to be drained by pumping. A mile and a quarter long and an average of fifty feet deep, the excavation required 300,000 pounds of gunpowder which at £2 10s. per cwt. cost £8,000. It is estimated that the whole operation cost about £200,000.

Ten miles beyond Roade we reach Weedon, then up Buckby Bank, across the Grand Junction Canal to Welton Station. With a warning shriek on the whistle we plunge into Kilsby Tunnel. It is 2,398 yards long, 28 feet high and 25 feet wide, with two huge ventilating shafts, each sixty feet in diameter, one of them 120 feet deep the other 90 feet.

The original contractor undertook to build the tunnel for £99,000 but the workmen struck a hidden spring which flooded the tunnel so rapidly that they only escaped by improvising a raft out of timbers which, it is said, one of the engineers towed to safety by means of a rope held in his teeth. The contractor gave up and died of a broken heart. Robert Stephenson carried on with the company's money. It took eight months of continuous pumping, night and day, at the rate of 2,000 gallons a minute and from a depth of 120 feet, before the quicksand spring was conquered and the tunnel finished. The total cost was £300,000, 36 million bricks were used to line the tunnel and 1,250 men, 200 horses and 13 steam engines were employed.

Out of Kilsby Tunnel we roll down a gentle slope into the town of Rugby, to stop at a station built in the style of a Swiss chalet. Then on across the Warwickshire countryside, where the leaves have not yet begun to fall, to Coventry. The spires of Grey Friars, Holy Trinity and St. Michael's (not yet a cathedral) dominate the skyline and soon we are in the station. Only eighteen more miles to go. We speed on through Hampton-in-Arden but before we

reach the Birmingham terminal we halt for a moment and a clerk of the railway company comes along the train to collect our tickets. A short while more and we have stopped under the roof of the station in Curzon Street. The $112\frac{1}{2}$ mile journey is over.

1 Entrance to the tunnel at Primrose Hill.
2 Entrance to the tunnel at Watford (the train here seems to be going backwards).
3 Wolverton Viaduct under construction.
4 The 'Great Ventilating Shaft' in Kilsby Tunnel.
5 Blisworth Cutting (there is a railway policeman, with signal flag, left).
6 The Birmingham terminus at Curzon Street.

RAILWAYS IN THE ARTS

FROM THEIR BEGINNING railways have exerted a strange fascination over people of all kinds. The fascination of something new, a machine which could draw men, animals and goods at twelve miles an hour, a contraption which enthusiasts saw as a means to all kinds of ends: economic, social and political. It was a challenge to the engineer, a speculation for the financier and to the general public a sometimes frightening symbol of a changing world.

The very scale of railway engineering caught the imagination and there was a popular demand for prints and drawings such as those in which J. C. Bourne recorded the construction of the London and Birmingham Railway and the Great Western Railway. Outstanding as pictures, Bourne's work also shows amazing technical accuracy and is a reliable record of those early years.

But there was more than engineering to attract the artist. The railway combined the elemental powers of fire and water—steam, speed, power—here was a stimulus few could resist.

To a painter like the English artist J. M. W. Turner who was working in terms of coloured light—what Constable called 'tinted steam'— here was a perfect subject. To anyone who thinks of railway travel on a stormy day as a depressing rain-washed window, Turner's *Rain, Steam, Speed* may seem a romantic overstatement; but another traveller, a certain Mrs. Simon, was able to confirm its truth. While travelling one rainy day, she was surprised to see the kindly looking old gentleman opposite put his head out of the window during a torrential downpour—and keep it there for nearly nine minutes! Then he drew back into the compartment, well and truly soaked, and sat with his eyes shut for another quarter of an hour. Mrs. Simon was so curious to know what had prompted this strange action that she put *her* head out of the window and was so fascinated that she too received a thorough drenching.

Next year she went to see the exhibition at the Royal Academy and overheard a visitor near by saying, 'Just like Turner, ain't it? Whoever saw such a ridiculous conglomeration?' Mrs. Simon looked at the picture he was talking about. It was *Rain, Steam, Speed*. 'I did,' she said.

During 1877 Claude Monet painted a series of pictures of the Gare St. Lazare in Paris. They show how the effects of steam and smoke must have interested this artist, who was so eager to record the changing effects of light.

The people and situations of railways have been the inspiration for many artists. Honoré Daumier produced a splendid series of railway drawings, full of character and incident. W. P. Frith, painter of the famous *Derby Day*, painted an equally animated scene set on the departure platform at Paddington Station.

Other artists were more interested in showing the excitement of the railway and suggesting the power of the locomotive. The American print-makers Nathaniel Currier and James Ives must have produced hundreds of coloured lithographs which combined dramatic effect with accurate representation of the railway. For more than fifty years their company produced about three prints a week on every aspect of American life. The lithographs were hand coloured on a mass-production system—one girl per colour—and they were in great demand all over the States and abroad. The same excitement has been caught, though perhaps with more sophisticated technique, by the modern English painter Terence Cuneo who has been particularly successful at evoking the fiery heat of the footplate and the pent-up energy of the steam locomotive. He has also been able to suggest the power behind the much less dramatic exterior of the diesel or electric locomotive. Much of Cuneo's work has appeared in posters commissioned by the railway companies.

Railway posters, whether depicting railway operations or places served by the railway— or in special designs to promote a particular service—have often led the way in poster design. London Transport in particular has produced designs of such high quality that many people wanted to hang them in their

---

1 Detail from W. P. Frith's *The Railway Station* (1862). The locomotive is the *Great Britain*, built in 1847.
2 Part of a poster by Terence Cuneo advertising a night freight service.
3 Third-class passenger travel, drawn by Honoré Daumier (1808-79).
4 The great train accident scene in *The Whip* (1909).
5 Illustration from the sheet music for *The Excursion Train Galop*, showing a South Eastern Railway excursion.

homes and copies had to be made available to the public. London Transport also led the way in commissioning work from sculptors Epstein, Gill and Henry Moore to decorate their headquarters building near St. James's Park.

Essayists have taken railways as their subject and poets have found railways an inspiration, and the railway has been the background to many plays from Ivanov's *The Armoured Train* and Afinogenov's *Distant Point* to *The Ghost Train*. Spectacular settings have ranged from the crash in *The Whip* in Victorian times to the Underground in Lionel Bart's *Blitz*.

Writers, dramatists and poets have all used the railway station setting. Apart from the steam, noise, crowds and atmospheric lighting which provide an excellent dramatic foil, a railway journey is a time between places, a time apart, and so to some extent is a railway station a place apart from the world around. It was for this reason that Jean Anouilh chose a provincial railway station for his setting of the Orpheus legend *Eurydice*. In Noel Coward's *Brief Encounter*, the refreshment room becomes a place outside society.

Massine based a ballet on the building of the Union Pacific Railroad, but *Terminal* merely used a station as a means of stringing a series of divertissements together and the Cocteau-Milhaud-Nijinska *Le Train Bleu*, named after the famous French train to the Riviera, was set on a bathing beach!

A railway journey gives the traveller an opportunity to reconsider, the writer a chance to ruminate or recapitulate. It can also throw people together without escape. A railway train has been a favourite setting for thriller-writers or film-makers.

The image of a great express rushing towards them was one of the first thrills for the kinematograph audience and America's earliest attempt at a narrative film was *The Great Train Robbery*, and anxious spectators in the nickelodeon would see Pearl White, or another favourite cliff-hanger heroine, tied to the rails with an express thundering round the bend. (But there is real tragedy in the death of Tolstoy's Anna Karenina beneath the wheels of a goods wagon.) From Hitchcock's *Strangers on a Train* to James Bond grappling with an enemy in *From Russia with Love*, the French resistance movie *The Train* or the zany humour of *The Great St. Trinian's Train Robbery*,

railways have been a gift to the film maker.

The cinema has also taken the story of the railroad itself and made such movies as Cecil B. de Mille's *Union Pacific*, the story of the building of the railroad, or John Ford's *The Iron Horse*, and of course the railroad played a major part in *The Way the West was Won*. The famous Civil War story of the locomotive called *The General* was used for Buster Keaton's classic film and retold by Walt Disney in *The Great Locomotive Chase*.

There have been several very fine films about railways. In 1944 Sidney Newman made *Trans-Canada Express* for the National Film Board of Canada, in 1960 John Schlesinger made *Terminus*, a film about a day on Waterloo Station, London, for British Transport Films, but probably the most famous of all railway films was made for the G.P.O. by Basil Wright and Harry Watt in 1935: *Night Mail*. This classic film has music by Benjamin Britten and specially written verse by W. H. Auden which reflects and continues the rhythm of the wheels on the natural sound track—the whole film is an exciting and romantic presentation of a mail train from London to Perth in Scotland.

Night Mail had a romantic treatment. Another exercise in combined documentary actuality, music and verse, this time in radio, did not. Ewan MacColl and Charles Parker's radio programme *The Ballad of John Axon* had an epic quality. Among the finest works ever devised for radio, this production from the B.B.C.'s Midland Region was inspired by the heroism of an engine driver.

Ewan MacColl's folk-song style music for this programme was in a long tradition of railway songs. In the United States in particular the railroad builders had sung their way

1 Buster Keaton in *The General*, the story of the *Great Locomotive Chase*.
2 A scene from *The Iron Horse*, directed by John Ford.
3 The *Coronation Scot* at speed.
4 Vittorio de Sica's *Stazione Termini* was set entirely within the confines of a railway station.
5 A lost child at Waterloo Station—in John Schlesinger's film *Terminus*, about a day at the station.
6 The British comedy *The Titfield Thunderbolt* (directed by Charles Crichton) told the story of an attempt to save a local line.

across the continent with ballads like *John Henry* and *Locomotive Bill* and railwaymen were celebrated in songs like *Casey Jones*. MacColl and Parker had been excited by Millard Campbell and Earl Robinson's radio ballad for *The Lonesome Train* but to this form they added actual recordings of people close to John Axon talking about the man and about life on the railway.

Work songs were not the only popular music to feature the railway. During the 1840's a piece called the *Excursion Train Galop* was extremely popular. There was an *Express Train Galop* too.

Many railways have found their place in popular songs. Crewe Junction has achieved fame less for its importance in the railway system of Britain than for its place in the music-hall song:

Oh Mr. Porter, what shall I do?

I wanted to go to Birmingham

And they've taken me on to Crewe.

Eric Coates' more recent *Coronation Scot* has a real feel of the railway about it.

It is not only lightweight composers who have found the railway interesting. Arthur Honegger, one of Les Six, in his *Pacific 231* written in 1923, has composed what must be the best-known musical work inspired by the railway. A quotation from an interview with Honegger which was published in the Geneva journal *Dissonance* forms a preface to the full score:

'I have always had a passionate liking for locomotives; for me they are living things, and I love them as others love women or horses. What I have endeavoured to describe in *Pacific 231* is not an imitation of the sounds of the locomotive, but the translation into musical terms of the visual impression and the physical sensation of it. It shows the objective contemplation; the tranquil breathing of the machine in repose, the effort to start, the progressive gathering of speed, leading from the lyric state to the pathetic, of a train of 300 tons hurling itself through the night at 120 miles an hour.

'For my subject I have chosen the locomotive type 'Pacific 231' for heavy trains of great speed.'

Honegger certainly succeeded in his intention. We feel the thrust of the powerful pistons, the driving rods beginning to move round with great force and then the free movement as the great locomotive speeds across the plains.

The Brazilian composer Heitor Villa-Lobos found inspiration in a very different train. A journey on a tiny Brazilian railway gave him the idea for his musical sketch *The Little Train of the Caipara*, a delightful, cheerful piece which he later incorporated in the second of his *Bachianas Brasileiras*.

Even Gioacchino Rossini, who refused to travel by train, wrote an amusing piano piece which he called *The Little Excursion 'Train*. One of the sections is headed 'The Derailment', which probably explains his dislike of railway travel.

The trains which inspired these composers —the big Pacific or the little Brazilian locomotive—were steam trains and the sounds which they evoke will soon be missing from many of our railways as the snort and hiss of the steam locomotive give way to the sound of the diesel and the rhythm of wheels over the joins in the track is lost as welded rail is laid. A railway journey will not sound the same; but these noises will not be lost, for enthusiasts in Britain and America have been carefully recording the sounds of the steam era and they are now available on gramophone records.

These recordings do not merely offer the exitement of an express train rushing stereophonically through your home (though you can have that too if you wish), the best of them really catch the railway atmosphere. Folkways in America and Transacord in Britain have issued some first-rate discs. As long ago as 1954 Peter Handford of Transacord set himself the task of recording as many steam locomotive types as possible before they were withdrawn. His aim is to record the railway's natural sound and he never asks a driver to produce spectacular effects; his sleeve notes too, help to create the exact atmosphere. One of his most exciting records, *Trains at Night*, must have involved many cold sessions waiting patiently by lonely stretches of track, but the results, recorded in stereo, are well worth while: we hear the locomotives slip on icy rails on a December night, we can feel the damp and smell the fog and hear not only the locomotives pounding past, or echoing off the hills, but the midnight owls, the signal levers, the fireman's conversation and the dawn chorus of moor and forest birds in the high fells.

1 *Rain, Steam, Speed,* by J. M. W. Turner (National Gallery, London).
Overleaf:
2 *Le pont de l'Europe, Gare St. Lazare,* by Claude Monet (Musée Marmottan).
3 *Le train dans la neige,* by Claude Monet (Musée Marmottan).
4 *The 'Lightning Express' Trains,* a Currier and Ives lithograph.
5 *The Return,* showing a first-class compartment, painted by Abram Solomon in 1855.

1

2

THE STORY OF CASEY JONES

Come all you rounders, I want you to hear
The story of a brave engineer,
Casey Jones was the rounder's name,
On a big eight-wheeler of a mighty fame.

Casey Jones, he pushed on the throttler,
Casey Jones was a brave engineer,
Come on, Casey, and blow the whistler,
Blow the whistle so they all can hear.

JOHN LUTHER JONES, from Cayce, Kentucky, was the original of the Casey Jones in the popular ballad. A fine railwayman, he was killed on 30th April 1900 when the train he was driving was wrecked at Vaughan, Mississippi.

On the evening of Sunday, April 29th, Casey and his fireman Sim Webb brought the No. 4 train from Canton into Poplar Street Station, Memphis, and were ready to go off duty; but the driver who was to take the No. 1 train south at 11.15 had reported sick and, since no other crew was available, Casey and Sim were asked to take over the trip.

No. 1 was an hour late getting into Memphis and another thirty-five minutes had been lost loading and switching before Casey was able to steam out of Poplar Street on his way south to New Orleans.

Jones was determined to make up the time. The locomotive ran beautifully and they were in Sardis in sixty-two minutes—thirty-five minutes already made up—by Grenada they had gained an hour. They sped on at speeds of over seventy miles an hour. They drew out of Winona only fifteen minutes late and at Durant were only five minutes behind: with only thirty-five miles ahead they would be in Canton on the scheduled time.

Ahead at Vaughan two goods trains had pulled off the single main track onto a double section to let Casey past, but together they were too long. A flagman was sent up-line and warning detonators set on the track to signal Casey that he was to 'saw by', that is cut speed and pull slowly down past the north points so that once he was clear the trains on the passing track could move north and clear the south end of the section.

At 3.50 a.m., only two minutes behind time, No. 1 swung into the long double 's' curve approaching Vaughan with the north set of points about the middle of the first 's'. As the train came rushing around the bend Sim Webb heard a detonator go off on the rail, and felt the air-brakes go on beneath his feet. Leaping to the right side of the cab he saw the flagman's lantern waving behind him, but ahead—where the first set of points should have been completely clear—were the red tail lights of a train on the main line. Casey could not see them because of the curve. Webb called out a warning and Casey told him to jump, pulled on the whistle and slammed on the emergency brakes. But it was too late.

They found Casey under the tender, still clutching the broken end of his whistle cord.

At the south end of the siding a local passenger train had drawn in with orders to get on the house-track at Vaughan station, out of the way of No. 1. But the points on to this track were blocked by the overhanging wagons of one of the goods trains. They had to pull north to let it through and as they moved back to clear the northern points for No. 1 an air-coupling broke bringing both trains to a stop. It was quickly replaced and pumping up the air pressure was begun but no one realised how fast No. 1 was running. Before they could get the remaining wagons off the main line Casey had ploughed into them.

Another wreck, another engineer dead—it had happened before on the railroad. But that was not the end of Casey Jones. Wallace Saunders and Ike Wentworth, railwaymen who had looked after Casey's engine at Canton, put their grief into a song which was soon being sung and whistled up and down all Mississippi with new verses being added day by day. By the time it was published in 1902 it was very different from the original version.

Nevertheless, however distorted the song may be it is still a great song of the railroad and gives lasting fame to Casey's name.

U. S. RAILWAYS TODAY
1 A gas-turbine-hauled goods train near Echo, Utah, on the Union Pacific Railroad.
2 A diesel-hauled train on the Chicago and North Western Railway which has double-decker carriages for commuter traffic. The locomotive operates on a push-pull basis; when pushing it is controlled from a cab in the forward coach.

THE BALLAD OF JOHN AXON

John Axon was a railwayman
To steam trains born and bred,
He was an engine driver
At Edgeley loco shed.
For forty years he followed
And served the iron way;
He lost his life upon the track
One February day.

At four a.m. that Saturday
John Axon left his bed;
At five he drew his time-card
At Edgeley loco-shed.
Just after six Ron Scanlon
His fireman, cried 'Away';
It was a day no different
From any other day.

The rain was gently falling
When they started down the line,
And on the way to Buxton
The sun began to shine.
From out the steam-brake pipe valve
A wisp of steam did rise,
And Axon he reported this
When in Buxton he arrived.

Under the large injector steam-valve
There's a length of one and one-eighth piping
Which connects with the driver's brake-valve.
The connecting point is a joint of brass.

A one and one-eighth steam-pipe
Fixed in a theaded joint,
Rests on asbestos packing,
And is sealed . . .
. . . sealed with brazing metal.

The repair was done and the train made up
When they left the Buxton sidings,
And the time was just eleven five
And the sun it was a-shining.

Four eight one double eight was her number
Scanlon was the fireman,
And the guard in the van was Alfred Ball,
And the driver was John Axon.

Her wagons numbered thirty-three,
And a twenty-ton rear brake van,
She was carrying coke, woodpulp and coal,
And firebricks and pig-iron.

The down line out of Buxton climbs,
She was pulling nice and steady,
And the bank engine was pushing behind,
And the guard's brake-stick was ready.

John Axon looked at the rolling hills
And he found them to his liking,
And he thought of his early courting days.
The days when he went hiking.

John Axon smiled at the thought that later
He'd be celebrating;
And he smiled when he thought of the Stockport pub,
Where a pint of mild was waiting.

John Axon was a dancing man,
On his pins he was light and nimble,
And often he'd stand on the old footplate
Whistling an olde-time jingle.

The joint of the driver's steam-brake pipe
Began to sweat a little,
By the time they were half way up the hill
It was coming in a steady trickle.

A hundred and twenty-five tons of engine,
Six hundred and fifty tons behind!
And the boiler pressure . . .
Two twenty-five pounds an inch!

And the men —
Two fragile bodies,
Flesh and blood,
And brittle bone.
Carbon and water,
Nerves and dreams.
Nerves and dreams.

Power from coal,
Power from water,
Power imprisoned
In a one and one-eighth pipe.

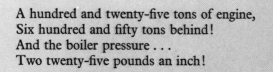

The restless steam
Watches the tired metal,
Explores the worn thread,
Watching,
Watching,

Every turn of the four-foot wheels
Every lunge of the smooth-armed piston,
Every thrust in the two great cylinders
Weakens the joint's resistance.

And the brazed flange crumbles,
The pipe is parted.
It **BLOWS!**

The engine had reached the distant signal
When the broken steam-pipe began to scream,
And John Axon and his mate couldn't reach the driver's brake,
For the cab was full of scalding steam, poor boys,
The cab was full of scalding steam.

*It was shock really, just for a few seconds. Then the realisation
came what had happened—that the brake pipe had gone. Conditions
on the footplate—oh! they was horrible. You only had to put your
face in and you'd have had it peel like an onion! (RON SCANLON)*

They hung on the side and they both took turns
At shifting the regulator from afar;
And they prodded at the bar with the pricker and the dart,
But they couldn't move the iron bar, brave boys,
But they couldn't move the iron bar.

John Axon he got to the fireman's side,
And over the scream of the steam did say
'We'll have to get outside if we want to stay alive
Or this'll be our dying day, poor boys,
Or this'll be our dying day'.

The guard he was waiting to pin down the brakes
The train it didn't slow down that day;
And he stood in the van with his brake-stick in his hand,
And he knew she was a runaway, poor boy,
He knew she was a runaway.

John Axon he cried to his fireman 'Jump!
It's the only thing you can do,
While I hang on the side and I'll take a little ride
For I've got to see the journey through, brave boy,
I've got to see the journey through'.

John Axon he was all alone, there on the engine side,
The train it reached the hilltop and began the downhill ride,
The sun it was still shining, the sky was still of blue,
He gambled with his life that day and this John Axon knew.

It's a seven-mile drop from Bibbington top,
O Johnny!
It's one in fifty-eight and you've no steam brake,
O Johnny!

She's picking up speed,
And the power is freed,
It's prayer you need,
But you'll never make it, Johnny!

Every yard of the track says you won't come back,
O Johnny!
She's a fist of steel, every turn of the wheels
Cries 'Johnny'!

There isn't a chance
You'll get to your dance,
You can see at a glance
That you'll never make it, Johnny!

There's a tunnel ahead, you can't cover your head,
O Johnny!
Doing sixty an hour and she's gaining power,
O Johnny!
Watch out for the wall,
Bunch yourself up small
In the smoky pall . . .
O, you'll never make it, Johnny!

It's hell on the plate, it's a funeral freight,
O Johnny!
It's the end of a dream in steel and steam,
O Johnny!
There's a world in your head,
And you're due at the shed,
And there's life ahead,
But you'll never see it, Johnny!

Every turn of the four foot wheels,
Every lunge of the smooth-armed piston,
Every thrust of the two great cylinders . . . .
Sings of a man's destruction.

What was it Jim said?
One day in the shed . . . .
Jim said . . . .
Or was it in the pub?
What was it that Jim said . . . .
About steam?
About power?

With a steam locomotive you make the
power, you direct the power and you control
the power.
You make the power, you direct the POWER
and you control the POWER.
CURSE the power!

The run it is finished,
The shift's nearly ended.
So long, mates!
So long . . . .
Remember
A man is a man
He must do what he can
For his brothers.

By his deeds you shall know him,
By the work of his hands,
By his friends who will mourn him,
By the love that he bore,
By the gift of his courage,
And the life that he gave.

On the 3rd May 1957 Mrs. Gladys Axon
received the following letter:

10 Downing Street,
Whitehall
2nd May 1957

Madam,

*I have the honour to inform you that the Queen
has been graciously pleased to approve the Prime Minister's
recommendation that the George Cross be awarded posthumously
to your husband John Axon . . .*

John Axon was a railwayman
To steam trains born and bred,
He was an engine driver
At Edgeley loco shed.
He was a man of courage
And served the iron way,
He gave his life upon the track
One February day.

*From THE BALLAD OF JOHN AXON, a radio
ballad by Ewan MacColl, Peggy Seeger, and
Charles Parker, first broadcast by the B.B.C.
Midland Region 2nd July 1958.*

THE END OF STEAM

THE DAYS of the steam locomotive are numbered. Steam power, to which the whole development of the railways was due, which has given them their shape and their emotional appeal, is inefficient when set against its successors.

Although initially diesel and electric locomotives cost much more than steam locomotives to build, they are much cheaper to operate. Not only are their fuel costs lower, they also require much less maintenance and therefore have a fuller working life.

From the time its boiler is lit, a steam locomotive needs three to five hours to build up sufficient steam power to be put to work. At the end of its trip, if it has been of any length, it must go into a depot to have its fire raked clear of ash and clinker and the smoke-box cleaned of soot. It will probably have to stop to be refuelled. At the end of the day the fire will be dropped, the engine allowed to cool and more maintenance work done. Then, at regular intervals, the engine's boiler has to be washed out. No matter how smoothly and efficiently these things are done, they all take time and staff. Time which, with a diesel or an electric locomotive, can be added to their working day, and staff who may prefer the cleaner working conditions of modern industry to the soot and grime that goes with coal-fired locomotives.

No, the electric- or diesel-hauled trains may seem coldly clinical to those of us who miss the dramatic atmosphere of smoke and steam, but they are cleaner and more efficient, and both they and their crews can complete far more traffic work. Steam has to go.

Coal, particularly the lower grades available today, is more effectively used at the power

1 One of the Union Pacific Railroad's 'Big Boys' hauling a long freight. These 132³/₄-feet-long 4-8-8-4s were built to handle fast freight traffic on heavy gradients at speeds up to 80 m.p.h. They rank among the greatest steam locomotives ever built.
2 A Class 241P four-cylinder comound of French Railways, equipped with mechanical stoker. Locomotives of this class were built between 1947 and 1949 for express passenger work.
3 The final development in French steamers was this Class U 4-6-4 four-cylinder compound passenger locomotive built in 1949.

1—6 (1) The first steam locomotive officially to record a speed of 100 m.p.h., *The Flying Scotsman,* built at Doncaster in 1923, here hauling its last train out of King's Cross before retirement on 14th January 1963. (2) A New Zealand-built 3 ft. 6 in. gauge 'K' type locomotive hauling a goods train near the top of the Spiral, Raumiru. (3) British Rail Class 9F 2-10-O, a versatile locomotive used mainly for heavy freight but also used for express passenger work. (4) A Merchant Navy class Bulleid heavy Pacific leaving Victoria with the *Golden Arrow*. This famous train is now electric hauled. (5) A West Country class light Bulleid Pacific. Locomotives of this class have the streamlining removed as in this picture. (6) The ultimate in German express passenger steam locomotives was this 4-6-2 No. 10,002; only two locomotives of the type were built (1956).

TRANS-EUROP-EXPRESS TRAIN-SETS
7 Swiss electric train-set. 8 German diesel train-set. This pattern has now been replaced by a standard German electric locomotive.

1 British Rail's diesel-electric type 4 number D 249.
2 Irish Railways' diesel-powered *Failte* express at Hazelhatch.
3, 4 British Rail's 3,300 h.p. electric locomotive for operation on 25,000 volts A.C. overhead supply.

3

4

1

2

station, generating electricity. And diesel power is the obvious choice where the capital cost, or other reasons, prevent electrification. The diesel power may be used either to drive an electric traction engine (diesel-electric) or the power may be passed on by hydraulic transmission, developed in Germany. Although electric transmission is more easily installed and maintained, hydraulic transmission is much less bulky—the weight saved can be added to the load hauled or the saving can be effected in lower fuel consumption.

Another choice for traction power is the gas-turbine, but gas-turbines work best when worked hardest, and if not required to work 'full-out' only give about the same ratio

JAPANESE NATIONAL RAILWAYS
1 Electric train-set for inter-city services.
2 Diesel car KI-HA 45000 for local services.
STEAM LOCOMOTIVES
3 An articulated Garratt locomotive by Beyer Peacock. The central boiler is free of all driving wheels and can therefore be bigger than is otherwise possible.
4 Union Pacific 4-8-4 Northern class.
5 Union Pacific 4-6-6-4 Challenger class.
6 New York Central Railroad Niagara S-10.
7 A Pennsylvania Railroad coal-burning locomotive powered by a steam-turbine instead of cylinders, pistons and driving rods. The engine and tender weigh nearly one million pounds and cover 123 feet of track.
8 A Franco-Crosti boilered locomotive of Italian State Railways. There is no chimney in the usual place; exhaust steam passes through the cylinders at either side of the boiler (which are in fact preheaters) and out through the stove pipes towards the rear.

ELECTRIC LOCOMOTIVES

1 The first electric train made by Werner Siemens in operation at the Berlin Trade Fair (1879).

2 Pennsylvania Railroad locomotive hauling the *Congressional*, operated daily in both directions between New York and Washington.

3 French Railways' locomotive, which operates on three different currents: 1,500 and 3,000 volts D.C. and 25,000 volts A.C.

4 New Haven Railroad two-unit 3,500 h.p. FL-9 locomotive which combines diesel and third-rail operation. Designed for routes which are only partially electrified, it can switch from one system to the other without loss of speed.

5 Swiss Federal Railways TEE train-set takes the 'Cisalpin' through the Rhône valley. This express links Milan, Lausanne and Paris in 8 hours.

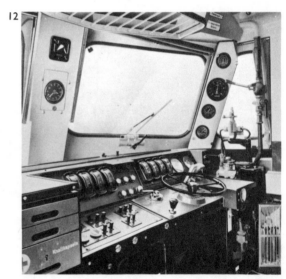

6 The *Golden Arrow* is now electric hauled on the third-rail system, but this locomotive has a pantograph which can take current from overhead supply in sheds and sidings.
7 A train-set operating on overhead supply on a Glasgow suburban service.
8 An E 646 locomotive of Italian State Railways.
9 An ALE 803 train-set in suburban service near Rome.
10 Italian State Railways' beautiful ETR 220 locomotive.
11 German State Railways' E 10 locomotive hauling the *Rheingold* express.
12 Inside the cab of the restyled E 10 locomotive.
13 A 3,600 h.p. D.C. locomotive in service with Spanish National Railways.

1

3

2

4

5

6

7

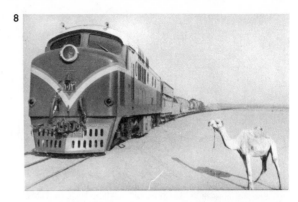

of work for fuel as a steam engine. They were tried out by British Rail but until recently only one railway system made much use of them — the Union Pacific Railroad, whose line between San Francisco and Chicago is particularly suited to their characteristics. Hauling heavy freight trains of up to 5,000 tons, locomotives climb to a height of 8,013 feet over a line which for 65 miles has a continuous gradient of more than 1 in 100. Under these conditions the locomotive is working full-out (and for technical reasons the cold air of these high altitudes makes for even greater efficiency). When the locomotive passes the high point of the route the gas-turbine is cut off and the train rolls down the long slope of the other side.

Now the ST6 gas-turbine, developed from an aircraft turbine, which overcomes many of the difficulties of operating at low speeds by using a free-power turbine, is being used in conjunction with lightweight rolling stock on the New Haven Railroad. The same turbine provides the motive power for Canadian National Railroad's 'Turbotrains', introduced in 1967 between Toronto and Montreal. Weighing only 250 pounds, and burning conventional diesel fuel, they are capable of developing 400 h.p. each. They can be started in temperatures as low as 60 degrees below zero and the Turbotrains are able to reach a speed of 100 m.p.h. within five minutes of starting. Designing on aerodynamic lines with many new features they look forward to the train of the future (see pages 150—1).

ELECTRIC LOCOMOTIVES
1 South African Railways' *Blue Train*.
2 A locomotive of Swedish Railways
7 French Railways' CC 40 100 class electric locomotive used for TEE Paris-Brussels-Amsterdam service.
DIESEL TRAIN-SETS AND
LOCOMOTIVES
3 A British Rail D 7000 class locomotive.
4 The *Torbay Express*, from London to the West Country.
5 British Rail Type 4 2,700 h.p. locomotive.
6 350 h.p. shunting locomotive being refuelled.
8 1,850 h.p. locomotive of Sudan Railways.
9 Queensland Government Railways' *Sunlander* express on the narrow-gauge route from Brisbane to Cairns, hauled by a 1,500 h.p. locomotive.
10 New South Wales train crossing Hawkesbury River Bridge.
11 2,000 h.p. train-set of Rhodesian Railways.

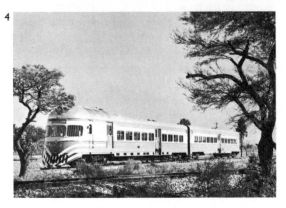

MORE DIESELS

1 A two-unit locomotive on the Moscow-Leningrad line, U.S.S.R.
2 Four GP-20 units provide 8,000 h.p. to speed this fast freight over the Montana Rockies.
3 A Baltimore and Ohio freight crossing the Susquehanna River.
4 A Fiat Type 131 rail car for Argentine State Railways.
5 A diesel-hauled passenger express of Canadian National Railways.
6 A locomotive of Italian State Railways.
7 A diesel-hauled train at Haifa, Israel.

GAS-TURBINE

8 One of Union Pacific's 8,500 h.p. gas-turbine locomotives hauling a heavy freight.

ATMOSPHERIC RAILWAYS

THE IDEA of propelling carriages by means of air pressure in an air-tight tunnel was proposed by George Medhurst in a pamphlet published in 1827 and an experimental system was tried out by a Mr. Vallance at Brighton but it had little popular appeal. The idea of being sucked through a dark tunnel was not attractive, particularly as Mr. Vallance proposed that his system should be used between London and Brighton.

Henry Pinkus, an American living in London, took out a patent in 1835 for a pneumatic system by which a piston pushed by air through a cylinder should propel a vehicle by means of a rod passing through a valve-sealed slit. He exhibited a model in Cavendish Square and the following year set up a full-scale trial. Others took up the idea and Samuel Clegg and Jacob and Joseph Samuda patented a version, with one edge of the valve fastened down, which they tried out at Wormwood Scrubs.

Various atmospheric railways, worked either by air pressure or vacuum, were proposed and lines were built for an extension of the Dublin and Kingstown Railway to Dalkey, for a line from New Cross (in London) to West Croydon, for a section of the Paris—Saint-Germain Railway, for a line between Geneva and Plainpalais

and for the extension of the Bristol and Exeter Railway to Plymouth.

The effect of wear and weather on the valves and other difficulties caused the system to be eventually given up, but not before it had been used for an underground Post Office railway in London. The first underground line in the United States, running 312 feet under Broadway from Warren Street, was also pneumatically operated.

1 & 2 An experimental pneumatic railway opened at the Crystal Palace, London, in 1846. These contemporary engravings show the starting of the train and its arrival at the other end of the tube.

FREIGHT AND ROLLING STOCK

Measures to speed freight and attract more custom to the railways include specialist bulk containers, like the 37,000 gallon tank car (10) the largest ever built to carry oil, 'piggy-back' arrangements carrying highway trailers on flat cars (9), 'flexi-vans' (1) and other types of road-rail containers, such as those used in British Rail's high-speed Freightliner service (5), and specialist services like the car-sleeper service for private motorists operated in Britain and on the continent (11). Increased efficiency is aided by modern automated marshalling yards (8), palettisation of loading (12), conveyor belts (4) and, in Europe, by the creation of a pool of wagons for international use through T.E.E.M. (6 and 7).

CABLE-WORKED RAILWAYS AND FUNICULARS

FIXED ENGINES and rope haulage were proposed for the Liverpool and Manchester railway until the success of the *Rocket* at the Rainhill Trials won favour for the locomotive. However, it was still thought impracticable for locomotives to manage steep gradients on their own and the system of endless rope haulage which had been used for many years in mines was adopted on some of the new railways and on the steeper parts of others, including the approach from Edge Hill to Liverpool and the rise from Euston to Camden Town on the London and Midland Line.

One of London's earliest railways, the London and Blackwall, was cable-worked for the whole of its $3\frac{1}{2}$ mile length; it was authorised in 1836 and Robert Stephenson and George Bidder were the engineers.

In 1841 the Düsseldorf-Elberfeld line was opened with a continuous incline of $1\frac{3}{4}$ miles cable-worked. Part of the Brussels-Liège main line was rope-worked for a section where the gradient is 1 in 32.

In the Peak District of England two of the nine cable-worked inclines which formed part of a line from Cromford to Whaley Bridge are still in operation.

London's first tube railway beneath the river from Tower Hill to Southwark was cable-operated, as was the Glasgow subway until electrified in 1935.

Until the 1930's there was a cable-worked railway at Jim Thorpe, Pennsylvania, the Mauch Chunk Switch-Back, which had originally been a coal-mine railway.

The most spectacular railway in the world with cable working must be one in South America: the Santos-Jundiai Railway of Brazil. The concession to build it was granted in 1856 and the line opened in 1867. Four cable-worked inclines each have a gradient of 1 in 9.75. To save expense one end of the hauling rope was attached to the ascending and one to the descending car, thereby reducing the power required from the stationary engines—a system used in funicular.

Funiculars, which are really ordinary rope railways worked on this principle over short steep gradients, are used all over the world whether to climb mountains, as in Switzerland, Norway or Japan, seaside cliffs as at Scarborough, Hastings, Folkestone and the Isle of Man, or just to climb steep hills as at

Montmartre in Paris or the Castle Hill at Bridgnorth.

Cable railways are by no means out of date: because of its steep gradient the underground railway recently built at Haifa in Israel is cable hauled.

1 A section of cable-operated track between Santos and Sao Paulo, Brazil.
2 The 'lifts' at Folkestone, Kent.
3 The cable car which connects the High Town and the Low Town at Bridgnorth, Shropshire.
4 The funicular at Montmartre, Paris.

MONORAILS AND SUSPENDED RAILWAYS

THE IDEA of self-supporting trains riding completely above the track was developed in the systems invented by Louis Brennan, August Scherl and Peter Schilovsky, which depend on gyroscopes to maintain equilibrium. If power failed the gyroscopes had sufficient momentum to keep their cars upright long enough for supports to be put in place or emergency rods with rollers to be lowered. Brakes could be applied for normal stops.

Brennan, an Irishman, was experimenting with monorails in 1896 and took out a patent in 1903, exhibiting a model in 1907. Scherl, a German pioneer, took out a patent in 1907 and gave a public demonstration of his car in the Berlin Zoological Gardens on 10th November 1909. Prior news of this reached Brennan, who quickly arranged a demonstration of his car for the same day followed by a more elaborate performance three months later. The invention excited great interest and won Brennan a Grand Prize when it was shown at the Japan-British Exhibition in 1910. The same year an agreement was drawn up which granted Scherl the right to use Brennan patents in Germany and to exhibit his car in the U.S.A.

Various systems of operation on a single rail had been developed, either with vehicles balanced by the man or animal pushing them along, by subsidiary supporting rails at the sides, or by carefully balanced panniers.

An alternative form of single-rail operation consists of suspending the train from the rail, and a horse-drawn form was in operation in London Docks as early as 1825.

A system of this kind invented by C. F. M. T. Lartigue was used for many years in North Africa. In 1894 an electrically operated Lartigue line was opened in Central France and others followed in Russia, Guatemala and Peru. An elaborate steam version was shown in London in 1886. In 1888 a $9\frac{1}{2}$ mile line was opened from Listowel to Ballybunion in Co. Kerry, Ireland, which ran successfully until 1924. The Managing Director of the Lartigue Railway Construction Company, Fritz Behr, developed the idea of a high-speed monorail and had a great success with a demonstration of his streamlined car at the Brussels Exhibition of 1897, and at the St. Louis World's Fair in 1904. There were plans for Behr railways between Liverpool and Manchester and between London and Brighton which eventually had to be dropped due to

1 The suspension railway at the Royal Panarmonion Gardens, St. Pancras, invented by a Mr. H. Torrington. 'The admittance to the Gardens is one shilling each person, entitling the parties to ride round the gardens in the car or on the Hobby Ho   Refreshments may be obtained on the premises.'
2 The demonstration of Scherl's monorail car in 1909.
3 A demonstration of the Brennan system in 1910.
4 Meigg's system proposed for an overhead railway in New York in 1886.
5 The Wuppertal Schwebebahn between Barmen and Elberfeld in Germany.
6 The *Skyway* monorail at Dallas.
7 The Safege system developed in France.

lack of capital and the opposition of the conventional railways.

A system particularly suited to underground railways was publicly presented by E. W. Chalmers Kearney in 1908, after six years of experiments. Trains ran on one rail with a second rail above the train to keep its balance. Kearney proposed that platforms could be sited immediately below the street, with a steep gradient to working depth which would assist acceleration on leaving a station and increase deceleration on coming into one. A railway was very nearly built beneath the Tyne between North and South Shields and there were proposals to use the system between Venice and the Lido and between Nice and Monte Carlo. The system was also suggested for an elevated railway in New York.

Of the many projects proposed for a suspended monorail the most important is that built and still in operation between Barmen and Elberfeld in Germany, the Wuppertal Schwebebahn, opened in 1901.

A British system invented by George Bennie, which combined the Wuppertal system with airscrew propulsion, was tried out in 1930. Economic and safe operation at speeds of 200 m.p.h. was claimed but despite various proposals for its development no regular service has been built on this system.

In the United States, Monorail Incorporated opened a test line for their Skyway system in Texas in 1956. An experimental saddle design was abandoned in favour of a suspended version which was built at the State Fair grounds in Dallas.

Two other systems seem the most likely to be developed in the near future: the Alweg system developed in Germany by the Swedish-born industrialist Dr. Axel Gren and the French Safege system.

A scaled-down experimental track and train of the Alweg saddle design were built near Cologne and demonstrated in 1952 and the first regularly operated track was opened at Disneyland, California in 1959. Another track was built with the co-operation of Fiat for

the Italia 61 Exhibition at Turin, and this system was also used for the mile-long link between Seattle and the Century 21 Exposition in 1962.

In the Safege system the car is suspended from pneumatic-tyred bogies, with carrying wheels and horizontal guide wheels (rather like those used on the Paris Mètro) which run within a hollow box girder. The designers claim to have developed a servo-mechanism which overcomes the tendency of suspended systems to sway. An experimental section of Safege track began operation near Orleans in 1960, and in 1966 work began on a line between Charenton and Creteil in the suburbs of Paris.

Monorails are being taken very seriously in Japan where a suspended system using bogies running *on top* of a supporting beam

has been developed. A line of this kind was built at Tokyo Zoological Gardens in 1957. A straddle system has been built in an amusement park at Nara and another straddle design, developed by the Lockheed Corporation of America, links the city of Nikko with the mountain resort of Kirifuri $2\frac{1}{2}$ miles away.

In 1964, in time for the Tokyo Olympic Games, an Alweg monorail, similar to that in Seattle, was opened between Haneda International Airport and central Tokyo. The train is carried on prestressed concrete beams 1.8 metres deep and 0.8 metres wide, cast in 10-20 metre sections. Two guiding wheels follow the track on top of the beam, two driving wheels operate horizontally on the sides of the beam and two other horizontal wheels act as stabilisers. All are pneumatic tyred and air sprung. Electric power is picked up from a track laid in the concave section on each side of the beam. The beam is supported by concrete pylons. The minimum radius of curves is 120 metres. Alweg claim that their trains can be used on slopes with an incline of 1 in 1 but the maximum on the Tokyo line is 6 in 10.

A monorail has often been proposed to link London airport with the city centre but the decision has continually been deferred and the building of a motorway link with west London puts it even further into the future.

1 The monorail built for the World Fair in Seattle.
2 The Tokyo-Haneda Airport line, the journey of over 13 kilometres takes 15 minutes.
3 The monorail at Nara.
4 The suspended monorail at Tokyo Zoo.

RAILWAY RELICS

In museums and collections all over the world all kinds of relics still survive to remind us of the colourful history of the railways.

1 An advertisement of 1833.

2 A warning to horse-cab drivers.

3 A china mug commemorating the opening of the Liverpool and Manchester Railway in 1830.

4 A section of Blenkinsop patent rack rail and wheel (1812).

5 Fish-bellied rail from the Stourton Tramway (1837), built from the original rails of the Liverpool and Manchester Railway.

6 Fish-bellied rails. This type of rail, used 1816—48, was made in four-foot lengths which clipped into connecting clogs.

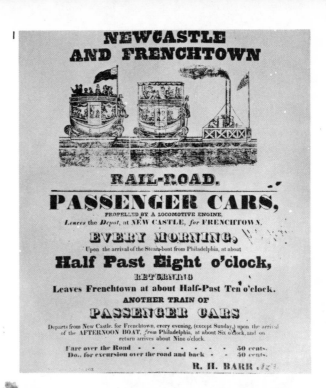

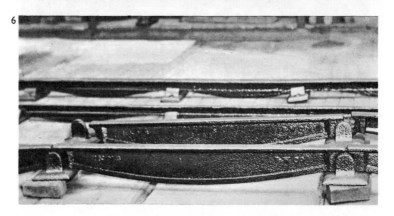

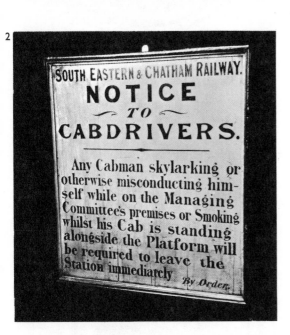

7

8

9

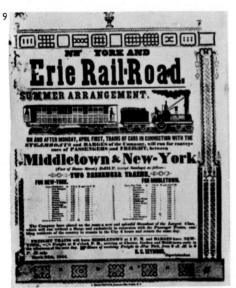

10

11

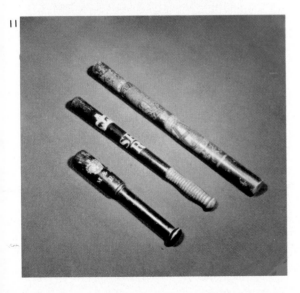

1—11 (1) Medal cast for the opening of the International Railway, Belgium and the Rhine (1843). (2) Ticket No. 1 on Canadian National Railways. (3) A pilotman's badge (the pilotman travelled on the footplate of all trains on a single track section) and an inspector's baton of office (the crown unscrews and his warrant was kept inside). (4) Station bell of 1836. (5) Station notice. (6) First signal lamp used on the Stockton and Darlington Railway (1840). (7) and (10) Rear and front lamps used on royal trains. (8) Headstock of Queen Victoria's 1869 saloon. (9) Poster of 1844. (11) Police truncheons of the Manchester and Liverpool and South Eastern Railways and a signal baton of the London and Birmingham Railway.

1 The Metropolitan Railway's steam locomotive No. 23, used on the Inner Circle Line. The pipes at the side of the boiler carried exhaust steam back to the water tanks where it was condensed.
2 A London Underground train at the platform at Bethnal Green Station.

UNDERGROUND RAILWAYS

WHEN AN URBAN TRANSPORT SYSTEM becomes inadequate and the streets are too congested to increase services, what is to be done? As London and New York grew in size and their populations mushroomed in the middle of the last century, people saw railways as a solution—but as there was no room to lay tracks in the streets the railway had to be overhead or underground.

In New York the Elevated Railway was first to be tried out (in 1867) but by then an underground railway had been in operation in London for more than four years. People had begun to make proposals for underground lines in London after the successful opening of a pedestrian subway beneath the Thames in 1843. By 1850 there was a crying need for a transport link between the main-line railway termini which were already handling a quarter of a million passengers a day. The answer was an underground railway from Bishop's Road, Paddington, to Farringdon Street via Euston and King's Cross.

In 1853 Parliament gave approval for the construction of the 3¾-mile-long line but work on its construction did not start until 1860. Most of the line was built by the 'cut-and-cover' method, following wherever possible the line of the existing street pattern. A great trench was dug down the centre of the street, the railway laid at its bottom and roofed with a brick arch and then the roadway relaid again on top.

On 9th January 1863, after a banquet at Farringdon Street, the Prime Minister, Mr. Gladstone, and members of the Cabinet travelled along the line in an open truck. The next day the Metropolitan Railway was opened to the public and carried 30,000 passengers.

Siemens's electric railway was still sixteen years away and this first underground was hauled by coal-burning steam locomotives. To keep the air as clean as possible these were designed to consume their own steam, which was passed into a condenser. The carriages, which earned the nick-name 'padded cells,' were lit by flickering oil lamps, passengers wanting to read on the journey would stick candles on the side of the compartments, but despite all the disadvantages 9,050,000 passengers travelled on the Metropolitan Railway during its first year. The Underground was successful and the lines were soon extended

north to Finchley Road, south to Kensington, east to Aldgate, west to Hammersmith. Another company was formed to build the District Line, and together the two companies created the Circle Line.

In New York in 1867 the editor of the *Scientific American*, Alfred Beach, was secretly tunnelling an Underground from a basement at the corner of Murray Street. Without bothering to obtain official permission he built New York's first subway, on which a single train was propelled by air pressure the 312 feet between Murray Street and Warren Street, under Lower Broadway. In 1869 the public were invited to try it out.

In 1870 a tunnel was cut beneath the Thames near the Tower for a rope-hauled railway of two foot six inches gauge. The seven-foot diameter tunnel was cut with a 'shield' developed by James Greathead from one Peter Barlow had patented in 1863. This could tunnel through the London clay and its invention made the cutting of deep 'Tube' lines a possibility.

In 1886 excavations began for the first deep-level 'Tube,' using the Greathead shield operated by hydraulic pressure. The three and a half mile line, known as the City and South London, linked the Monument north of the Thames with London Bridge Station and Stockwell to the south. The original plan was that the trains should be cable-hauled but before the tunnel was completed it was decided that they should be electrically driven. The City and South London was opened in 1890. It now forms part of the Northern Line. Other tube lines followed, including the famous 'Tuppeny Tube,' the Central London Railway from Shepherd's Bush to the Bank which was opened in 1900. The smoke-free 'Tubes' proved stiff competition for the underground lines and these were gradually converted to electric traction. The whole of London's underground and tube railways are now part of the London Transport underground system except for the line linking the Bank and Waterloo Station (opened in 1898), which is operated by the Southern Region of British Railways, and the completely independent Post Office Tube Railway used exclusively for the transfer of mails between the London District Offices, which is automatically operated.

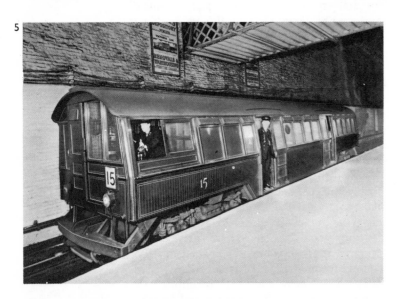

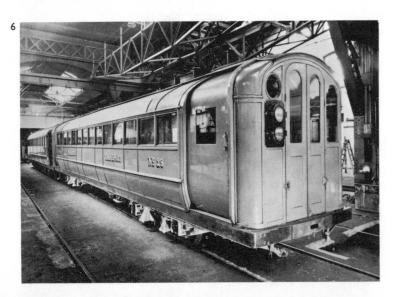

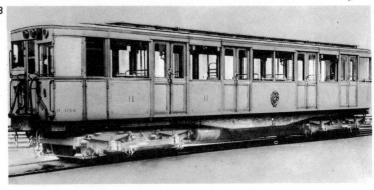

The first underground railway on the European continent was the Franz Josef Electric Underground in Budapest, opened in May 1896. Two miles long, it was the first Underground to be given a flat roof. Built by the 'cut-and-cover' method, the double-track tunnel is rectangular with central supports.

The next city to have an Underground was Glasgow, where a circular line in two concentric tunnels was begun in 1891 and opened in January 1897. Until 1935 the motive power consisted of endless wire ropes which were gripped by the carriages. They were driven by static steam engines which gave the ropes a speed of 15 miles per hour. Electric working was substituted in 1935.

In 1898 a one and a half mile long cut-and-cover line was built under Tremont Street, Boston. Although it was originally used by street-cars only, it was America's first public subway line. In Europe that same year the Stadtwerk system was opened in Vienna with steam traction and work was begun in Paris on the Métro. In July 1900 the first section, from Porte Vincennes to Porte Maillot, was opened to the public. This ten-kilometre line linked the Place de la Bastille, the Louvre, the Place de la Concorde, and the Arc de Triomphe. The engineer, M. Bienvenue, and the contractor, M. Chagnaud, used their own version of the cut-and-cover system to build the line. They excavated from the street down to the planned roof level, built the roof, replaced the street and then constructed the underground underneath the roof.

In 1902 the U-Bahn was opened in Berlin, the first section from Potsdamer Platz to the Zoo having only 2.3 kilometres in tunnel, the rest being on viaducts.

In March 1900 work had started on New York's first public subway line from City Hall to Grand Central, Times Square and West 145th Street. Long before the line was finished approval was given to extend it out to Brooklyn and contracts were being invited for other lines. The official opening was on 27th October 1904 when the first train pulled out of City Hall full of city notables.

Philadelphia followed with $4\frac{1}{4}$ miles of Underground in 1908. Hamburg opened a circular line, of which about a quarter was underground in 1912. In 1913 a completely underground line was opened in Buenos Aires.

Since then more and more cities have seen underground systems as a necessary addition to their transport services: Madrid (opened 1919), Barcelona (1924), Sydney (1926), Tokyo (1927), Moscow (1933), Osaka (1933), Chicago (1943), Stockholm (1950, the first tunnel converted from a tramway system), Toronto (1954), Rome (1954), Leningrad (1955), Cleveland, Ohio (1956), Nagoya (1957), Lisbon (1959), Haifa (1959, cable hauled), Kiev (1960), Milan (1964), Montreal (1966). There are several other cities where conventional railway or tramway systems have sections underground: Brussels, for instance, has a two-kilometre tunnel section six tracks wide linking the two mainrail termini. Copenhagen, Liverpool, Oslo, Warsaw and San Francisco all have sections underground.

Undergrounds are being built in Baku, Tbilisi, Washington and Rotterdam and lines are projected in many other cities; meanwhile the older lines are being continually extended. The Paris Métro, for instance, is building a new express line between St. Germain-en-Laye and Boissy-St. Leger, and London Transport will add 10½ miles to the 258-mile route length of its system when the new Victoria line is completed.

Underground development has by no means been limited to extensions of track. Efficiency of operation and comfort have been continually increased. Methods of construction have advanced and rolling-stock has changed enormously. The 'padded cells' of the early London Underground have given way to lightweight aluminium carriages with comfortable seats and automatic doors. Automation has been introduced everywhere from the ticket-vending machines the escalators and automatic lifts to the destination indicators, the automatic signalling and the 'programming machines' which control the automatic signalling of several sections of the London Transport system. These carry information of the train service as a series of punched holes on a roll like that of an old fashioned pianola. The coded information is 'read' by a row of feelers and signals and points are set automatically according to the

existence, or lack, of a hole. As each train leaves the section controlled by the machine it moves the roll on a line. Should a delay cause a train to get out of schedule a 'time-machine,' similar to the programming machine, but with an information sheet moving according to the official timings, works in operation with the programming machine to put through another train if necessary and then signal the first train through out of schedule. If trains get very much out of order the central control room is automatically informed and human operators can take over on push-button controls

In New York one public line is already completely automatic. A shuttle service between Grand Central Station and Times Square is operated with driverless trains operated by electronic signals passed along the rails.

The Paris Métro has introduced pneumatic-tyred trains on its No. I and No. II lines. Pneumatic tyres are claimed to give much smoother running and, by improving the adhesion of the motor bogies, increase acceleration and braking, thus cutting journey times and increasing route capacity. The tyred wheels are mounted outside the normal flanged wheels and are a little larger. Horizontal wheels also press sideways against a side rail. At points and cross-overs the running surface of the pneumatic wheel drops, lowering the flanged wheel onto the normal rails.

Surface congestion has led to the construc-

1—10 (1) Lifts and escalators are an essential part of all underground systems. This one is in Stockholm. (2) The vestibule of Electrozavodskaya Station, Moscow. Many of the Moscow Metro stations are lavishly decorated. (3) Tunnelling work on London's Victoria Line. (4), (6) and (8) Carriages from Buenos Aires, New York and London. New York caters for more standing passengers, Buenos Aires has no straphangers. (5) and (7) The London Post Office Railway driverless trains are controlled by switching on and off the current. The mail bag containers roll on and off the cars. (9) The guard's controls on a London Underground train. He is in microphone contact with the driver (panel, right) and controls the doors by push-buttons. (10) Programme machines on London Underground.

SIGNALS

tion of more and more passenger lines, but as long as urban conditions include rush-hour transport peaks that require the provision of rolling-stock and staff that are used for only a small part of the day, these and high construction costs mean that the Underground must be viewed as a public service rather than a commercial undertaking. Many routes lose money, but far less than the transport snarl-ups they prevent would cost. Perhaps the day will come when transport, like streets, will be considered a necessary provision to be paid for from the public purse. A survey of the Paris Métro showed that the cost of selling tickets and checking passengers was greater than the income from fares—it would be cheaper to operate the Métro free.

On some systems, in Paris, New York, Moscow and Rome for instance, there is a standard fare payable whatever the distance travelled; on others, such as the London Underground, the fare is proportionate to the distance travelled. Each system seems to have its own peculiarities and it is as well to discover them — many American visitors to London, for instance, will have been surprised to find they should have kept their ticket to give up at the end of their journey (this applies to surface railway travel too). In London you buy a ticket from the ticket office or an automatic vending machine and may be asked to show it for the whole length of the journey. In Paris you buy a ticket or, to save money and time, a block (*carnet*) of tickets from the ticket office and may be asked to show it to an inspector on the journey but do not have to show it at the exit. The Métro has both first- and second-class carriages. In New York you buy a token from the subway office and put it in a turnstile to get into the subway. On the Roman Metropolitana you buy a token from a stand which also sells newspapers and magazines and put it in a turnstile which issues a paper ticket.

One system for which you can never buy a ticket is the Post Office underground railway in London, for it carries no passengers, only mail bags. It has no drivers, and is controlled by the switching on and off of the power supply.

Without their signs underground platforms would be difficult to tell apart: 1 Paris. 2 Stockholm. 3 Berlin. 4 Tokyo. 5 Toronto. 6 Moscow. 7 Chicago. 8 New York.

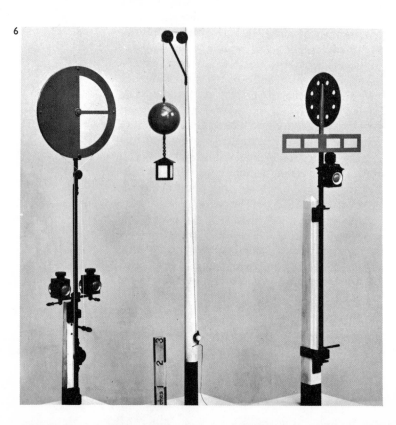

The safety of a railway depends upon careful maintenance and efficient signalling. Signal forms have changed a great deal from the policeman with a flag to the automatic systems of today.

Preceding page Station post signal (1844) set at caution and danger.

1 Railway policemen (1844). The flag position left indicates slacken speed because of a defect in the rails, that right slow down — another train ahead.

2 Forty signals at stop. The biggest gantry in Britain (1934).

3 Modern colour-light signals.

4 Upper quadrant distant signal at clear.

5 Ground disc signals.

6 Models of revolving disc signal (London and South Western Railway, 1840), ball signal (Great Western, 1837) and disc and crossbar signal (Great Western, 1841).

ELEVATED RAILWAYS

ELEVATED RAILWAYS were the obvious alternative to Undergrounds for city transportation. They found favour because they were much cheaper to construct and because it was thought that Undergrounds would damage the foundations of buildings which they passed beneath.

By the mid-1850's people were proposing overhead railways for New York, horse-drawn, rope-hauled, atmospheric, suspended—but it was not until July 1867 that the money was found for the first experimental track, from Greenwich Street, Manhattan, up Ninth Avenue to 30th Street. In December that year the inventor, Charles Harvey, made the first trip on the world's first elevated track. In 1868 the State Commissioners and the Governor approved the venture and the system was rapidly extended.

In 1893 the overhead railway along the Mersey shore in Liverpool became the first elevated railway to use electric traction.

The drawbacks of the Elevated running through city streets and the increasing development of Undergrounds led to the system losing favour and the Liverpool Overhead and most of the New York system have now been dismantled. In recent years there has been a renewal of interest in overhead monorails, such as the one built for the Century 21 Exposition at Seattle, particularly as links between airports and city terminals.

1 The 'El' near the waterfront in 1884.
2 A trial trip on the first elevated railway (1867).
3 On Third Avenue near 10th Street.
4 The Liverpool Overhead Railway, opened in 1893, was the first to use electric traction.

A GLIMPSE OF THE FUTURE

'RAILWAYS ARE FINISHED as a means of transport.' What utter nonsense! The railways were developed before the invention of the internal combustion engine and the aeroplane but that does not make them obsolete now. The railways cannot compete with the supersonic speeds of jet aircraft or with the door-to-door manoeuvrability of the family motor-car, but they can offer much greater safety and comfortable direct travel from city centre to city centre. Even with the development of vertical take-off it seems unlikely that airports will ever be sited in a central, easily accessible position, and the strain of driving cannot be removed from the private motorist.

Many railways have lost ground in the economic field. Saddled with heavy upkeep costs for permanent way and depot facilities, often with accumulated debts and committed by law in many cases to run uneconomic services, they must compete with road services having minimal overheads. But think what a railway train can do—haul hundreds of sleeping passengers and thousands of tons of freight, in safety and at speed, almost regardless of weather and with a single driver, instead of the innumerable lorries or motor-coaches which would otherwise be required.

As the world's industrial conurbations grow ever larger and traffic congestion increases, transport planning will become imperative, and in many areas efficient and frequent public services may replace the one-man-one-vehicle attitude prevalent today. If placed on an equal footing with other transport methods the railways will be able to offer an incomparable service wherever regular, large-scale transport is required, and a service which modern technical developments are daily improving.

What changes are these technical developments bringing about on the railways themselves?

Steam will be replaced, first by diesel or electric power, then perhaps, much farther in the future, by atomic power.

Speeds will increase, and this will mean that track will be laid or relaid straighter (though a slight curve makes the wheel flange press against the side of the rail and increases safety).

Bends there still will be, and when rounding bends at high speeds vehicles tend to be pushed outwards by the centrifugal force. This could be countered by sloping the track inwards, as on a motor-racing circuit, but to do so would cause considerable difficulties where slow traffic used the same line, or if a train had to stop on the curve. The strain placed upon the inner rail makes a super-elevation of six inches the maximum possible.

American engineers were working on this problem in the early 'forties and devised a carriage called the 'Precopendulum' which inclined as it rounded corners in the same way as a cyclist leans when going round a corner on a bicycle. In this carriage the inclination was obtained by using flexible springs, but in 1957 French Railways built an experimental prototype of a pendulum carriage with two bogies on which the body could oscillate. The body was built on to a steel girder, each end of which was shaped like a swan's neck and the ends of the girder rested on raised supports on the bogies.

1 French Railways' 'pendulum' train.
2 Enormous lengths of rail for welded track are themselves a tricky transport problem.
3 One of the super-expresses on the new Tokaido line, Japan. Capable of 130 m.p.h. they complete the 320 mile journey at an average speed of 101 m.p.h.
4 The suspension system on Canadian National Railway's Turbotrains which banks cars inwards on curves instead of outwards. The solid line shows the position on a curve, the dotted line the train on level track.

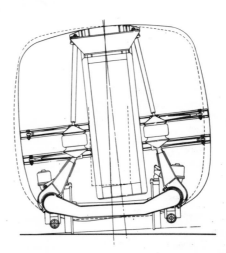

1 Pennsylvania Railroad's 'hot box' detector is so sensitive that it can detect the warmth of a human hand 200 yards away. An overheated bearing on a passing train causes a sudden leap to be marked on a linked graph roll at the signal box.

2—4 Television used on the Paris Ligne de Sceaux to enable station staff to see the whole length of a long curving platform (2), in the remote control of a level crossing on French Railways (3) and to identify numbers of freight trucks in the U.S.A. (4).

5 An electronic brain at Elkart, Indiana, which 're-members' and supplies information on each freight car, or group of cars, during marshalling.

Canadian National Railroad's new Turbo-trains use a pendulum system which, combined with a guided axle system and a low centre of gravity (floors are 10 inches lower than in their usual rolling-stock) give smoother riding. Carriage building of this kind will make sure that fast travel is still comfortable travel for the passenger.

Locomotives are becoming more powerful and, as more powerful locomotives haul heavier loads, it may become necessary to resort to a wider gauge. The Soviet scientist, Professor Vassili Vassilievich Zvonkov, considers the Russian 1.524 metre gauge already inadequate and 9—15 feet gauges necessary to allow for roomier trucks, 40—50,000 h.p. locomotives and speeds from 150—200 m.p.h. He thinks even wider gauge tracks across the Continent may prove necessary in later years.

Electrical traction and steel rails make the railway an ideal subject for automation and remote control. Instructions can be transmitted along the metals themselves. France, Germany, the U.S.A. and the U.S.S.R. have all made successful experiments in radio control. New York Subway already has one automatic shuttle service and London Underground a section of automatic signalling controlled by a programming machine.

Modern colour light signalling has already made the semaphore old-fashioned and the installation of various types of Automatic Warning Systems has increased the effectiveness of signalling by reproducing signal information in the driver's cab and automatically applying the brakes if it is ignored.

Low currents passed through the running

6 The control panel at Old Oak Common signal box.
7 Mills propane gas heaters at York station stop points from freezing.
8, 9, 10 The induction equipment of British Rail's Automatic Warning System (8) foreground, is connected with the signal seen ahead. Through the magnet carried beneath the locomotive (9) it activates the striped dial and the bell within the cab (10) and automatically applies the brakes if they are ignored.
11 A British Rail automatic carriage-cleaning plant.

rails of a section of track (each section being insulated from the next) are short-circuited by the wheels and axles of passing trains. This can be used to stop signals being cleared behind the train, or points being changed in front of it. To go a stage farther, it can actually operate the signal behind it, clearing the signal as the train passes out of the section, and it can operate level crossings in the same way. Track circuiting also operates a series of lights along the track diagram at signal boxes to show the signalmen the position of the train. By a code system of letters and numbers, which can be set at the train's point of origin and automatically transferred to signal-box diagrams along the route, the train can be identified by the signalman in charge. These train description codes can also be used to automatically set the correct route ahead of the train by incorporating a symbol indicating the required route.

In Germany half the mileage of the Federal Republic's rail system is controlled by Automatic Train Control. This not only applies the brakes if the driver passes a distant signal at caution without pressing a button to disengage the mechanism, but will also apply them if he does not reduce speed to 56 m.p.h. within 22 seconds of passing the signal, if the train is travelling at more than 41 m.p.h. 160 yards ahead of the home signal, or if the train overruns the home signal. With this system trains cannot overrun a stop signal by more than one-eighth of a mile, even if travelling at 100 m.p.h. when the A.T.C. comes into operation.

Different frequency impulses passed through the running rails can be used to transmit varied information. On the Pennsylvania Railroad where the breaking of the circuit when a locomotive passes sends electric messages back along the track to set the previous signal, the frequency is raised and sets the signal before that to the right position, increasing the frequency at each signal until it reaches a level at which it sets a signal clear. This information is also picked up by the locomotive and shows the setting of other signals ahead.

In 1955 French Railways began experiments with radio-controlled, driverless trains with locomotive BB. 9003, of the same type as the rail-speed record-holder. From a diesel railcar on a parallel track orders to release brakes,

control the supply of current to the traction motors of the locomotive and apply the brakes at the end of the run were given verbally by radio-telephone to a radio-control post. From there signals were sent out to the receiving set on the locomotive, which in turn set the necessary mechanisms in motion.

The aerial on the train was quite short, the receiving set very light in weight and the relay could be placed in the waistcoat pocket. Starting and acceleration up to maximum speed are automatic on this type of locomotive and the only things which had to be operated by remote control were the brakes and the supply of current. This system did not even use the rails to transmit signals.

British Rail have been experimenting with a system where two conductor wires are laid between the rails and connected to an alternating current source. One is parallel to the rails, the other follows a zig zag which varies in length of wave according to the speed required on that section of track. Induction from one wire to the other creates a magnetic field and the effect of the zig zag is to vary its intensity along the line of movement. As the locomotive runs along the track this fluctuation is picked up as pulses increasing or decreasing according to the length of wave—and apparatus on the train causes it to brake or accelerate. A refinement uses a square-wave in binary code.

Many countries are experimenting with the use of compuutors, both in the locomotive and at central control. (They are, of course, already an essential part of the administrative apparatus of many railway systems.)

Illogically, many people seem to prefer a fallible human driver to an almost infallible machine which, if it fails, automatically fails safe—it stops—but the problem of the future is likely to be a different human one. The driver travelling on an automatic train will have nothing to do unless there is a breakdown. Will it be possible to find a person capable of coping with an emergency situation who will be able to tolerate the boredom of normal running? However they develop, railways in the future are going to be very different from those we have known for the last hundred years. Dr. Sydney Jones of British Rail looked forward in these words:

We can envisage a transport system which

would be capable of speeds of 200 and 300 m.p.h. on track that was largely if not entirely separate from existing railway track, running on silent steel wheels and signalled by a continuous system of communication between the train and control. The track construction would probably be different from the conventional railway, the construction techniques embodied in vehicles would be similar to those found in aircraft practice, and the shape would be dictated by aerodynamic considerations to reduce the drag at full speed. 'The tractive power would probably be electric, and at these speeds the linear could well come into its own ... Such a transport system would no longer have to be compatible with conventional railways, and the railway designers would for the first time be free from the straightjacket which has inhibited innovation in the railway.'

1 Canadian National Railroad's *Turbotrains* combine aluminium structure, pendulum suspension and a low centre of gravity with guided axles and gas-turbine engines to create a very fast and very comfortable train.
2 The *Talgo* train, a Spanish development, is an articulated whole with the front end of each trailer resting on the rear end of the preceding coach. The wheels supporting the rear maintain an imaginary axle at right-angles to the longitudinal axis and the carriage surrounds them, giving a low centre of gravity. This form of suspension enables a higher speed at curves than is possible with an ordinary train.

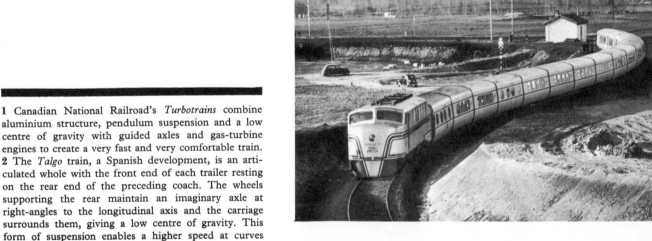

3 The train of the future? Research prototype for a *Limpet* (linear induction motor propelled train), developed by Professor E. R. Laithwaite of Manchester University and British Rail's Research Department. A vertical metal plate along the centre of the track is sandwiched by the windings of the motor. Current from overhead is supplied to the motor windings in three-phase form, corresponding currents are induced in the plate and the reaction between the two propels the train along the track. Tractive effort is not limited by adhesion and there are no moving parts, so both acceleration and braking (by reversing the current) are much greater than in other land vehicles. Running speeds up to 200 m.p.h. are possible.

ACKNOWLEDGMENTS

The author and publishers are indebted to the Central Office of Information for permission to reproduce W. H. Auden's verses from the film *Night Mail* and to the writers and the British Broadcasting Corporation for the extracts from *The Ballad of John Axon,* which was the first of a series of radio ballads written by Ewan MacColl and Peggy Seeger, and edited and produced by Charles Parker, Senior Features Producer in the B.B.C.'s Midland Region. Our thanks are also due to Mrs. Gladys Axon, Mr. Alec Watts, Mr. Jack Pickford, Mr. Roy Howarth and Mr. Ron Scanlon. This radio programme has now been issued on a gramophone record by Argo Records. *London to Birmingham 1836* is based on material supplied by British Rail. (London Midland Region). *The Story of Casey Jones* includes material supplied by Mr. Jim Sullivan of the New York Central System.

We should also like to thank the staff of the Museum of British Transport and the many railway companies throughout the world who have given assistance in the preparation of this book, and the following for permission to reproduce illustrations. (Figure in roman type is page on which caption appears, figure in **bold** is number of illustration).

Ab Stockholm Sparvägar 140 **1**, 142 **2**
Alaska Railroad 91 **3**
Association of American Railroads 33 **3**, 35 **1**, 55 **9**, 80 **1—3**, 87 **5**, 89, **5** 127 **11**, 133 **1**, 135 **9**
Atchison, Topeka & Santa Fé Railway 67 **8—10**
Australian News and Information Bureau 39 **1**, 45 **5**
Baltimore & Ohio Railroad 61 **2**, 84 **1, 7**, 124 **3**
B. T. Batsford Ltd. 77 **3** (from *British Trains* by O. S. Nock)
Berliner Verkehrs-Betriebe 142 **3**
Black Star 130 **7**, 132 **1**, 45 **2** (*John Launois*)
British Rail 13 **4**, 14 **2**, 19 **2**, 21 **1**, 22 **2**, 24 **2**, 49 **1, 3**, 53 **3**, 56 **1, 4**, 64 **3—6**, 73 **2**, 77 **1—2**, 78 **2—4**, 81 **1**, 82 **1, 2, 4—6**, 84 **3, 8, 10**, 87 **4**, 89 **2, 7—8**, 91 **3**, 92 **1**, 95 **4—6**, 97 **1—6**, 98 **2, 5**, 101 **3**, 110—111, 114 **3—5**, 116 **3—4**, 120 **6—7**, 123 **3—6**, 127 **4—5, 9**, 133 **3—4**, 135 **4, 6**, 148 **1, 7, 9, 11, 13—15**, 150 **3—7**
British Transport Films 101 **5**
Maurice Broomfield 116 **3**
Camera Press 30 **8**, 74 **2**
Canadian National Railways 89 **13**, 91 **7**, 124 **5**
Canadian Pacific Railway 45 **3**, 69 **6**, 70 **2**, 127 **10**
Central Press 53 **2**
Chicago Transit Authority 142 **6**
Cie. Internationale des Wagons-Lits 61 **5, 8, 10**, 62 **1—6**
Delaware & Hudson Railroad 33 **4**
Deutsche Bundesbahn 50 **1, 3**, 69 **2—3, 8—9**, 70 **5**, 89 **9—10**, 114 **6, 8**, 120 **4**, 121 **11**, 127 **12**, 148 **8, 12**
East African Railways & Harbours 45 **6**
English Electric 46 **1**, 89 **14**, 121 **5**, 123 **1, 7—8, 10**
F.I.A.T. 69 **5**, 124 **4**
Ferrovie dello Stato Italia 69 **1**, 70 **4**, 78 **7**, 87 **3, 8—11**, 89 **1, 12, 15**, 91 **1—2**
H. G. Forsythe 144 **3, 4**
French Embassy 28 **4**
C. L. Fry 116 **2**
Giraudon 103 **2—3**
Glasgow Corporation Transport 138 **6**
Great Northern Railway 67 **1—7**, 124 **2**
Gulf Oil Co. 33 **2**
H. M. Postmaster-General 49 **2**, 140 **5, 7**
High Commissioner for New Zealand 114 **2**
Israel Tourist Office 124 **7**

Japanese Embassy 130 **8**, 132 **2**
Japanese National Railways 119 **1—2**
Järvägsmuseum, Stockholm 78 **5**
Chas. E. Keevil 73 **3**
Keystone 116 **1**
E. R. Laithwaite 150 **1**
London Transport Executive 138 **3**, 140 **8—11**
Raymond Mander & Joe Mitcheson Collection 98 **4**
Mansell Collection 10 **1**, 26 **3**, 28 **2**, 30 **5**, 35 **2**, 39 **3**, 40 **3**, 43 **2**, 61 **1**, 64 **1—2**, 84 **2**, 87 **2**, 91 **5**, 98 **3**, 103 **4**, 125 **1—2**
John Masey-Stewart 74 **3**
J. Meredith 53 **6**, 74 **4**, 130 **4**
Mobil Oil Co. 127 **3**
Mount Washington Cog Railway 53 **5**, 55 **4**
Musée Marmottan (Giraudon) 103 **2—3**
Museum of British Transport 78 **1**
Museum of the City of New York 142 **10** (J. Clarence Davis Collection)
Mustograph 10 **4**, 13 **3**, 19 **1**, 55 **5**, 81 **2**, 84 **6**, 128 **2—3**, 133 **5**, 145 **4**
Nairn's Photo Services 46 **3**
National Gallery, London 103 **1** (Photo: M. Holford)
New York, New Haven & Hartford Railroad 120 **4**
New South Wales Government 30 **6**
New York Central System 87 **7**, 119 **6**, 127 **1**, 148 **5**
New York City Transit Authority 138 **11**, 140 **6**, 142 **7**
Norfolk & Delaware Railroad 50 **2**
Norges Statsbane 46 **5**
Novosti Press Agency 140 **3**
Österreichische Bundesbahnen 30 **4**
Pennsylvania Railroad 35 **3**, 55 **3**, 87 **1**, 89 **4, 6**, 119 **7**, 120 **2**, 150 **2**
Paul Popper 28 **1**, 30 **1**, 45 **1**, 55 **5**, 73 **1**, 130 **6**, 132 **2**, 138 **10**
Radio Times Hulton Picture Library 10 **3**, 13 **1**, 21 **2**, 24 **1—3**, 26 **1—2**, 30 **3, 7**, 33 **1**, 39 **4**, 43 **3—5**, 45 **4**, 53 **4**, 55 **2**, 61 **3**, 70 **1**, 78 **6**, 84 **4**, 101 **1**, 120 **1**, 128 **1**, 130 **1—3, 5**, 133 **6**, 138 **1**, 142 **8—9**, 144 **2**
Red Nacional de los Ferrocarriles Espanole 148 **6**
Regie Autonome des Transports Parisiens 128 **4**, 138 **8—9**, 142 **1**, 148 **2**
Lewis Robertson 74 **1**
Schweizerische Bundesbahnen 70 **3**, 92 **5**, 114 **3**
Science Museum, London 5, 9 **1—2**, 10 **2**, 13 **2**, 14 **1**, 16 **1—4**, 22 **1**, 55 **3, 6**, 82 **3**, 89 **3**, 138 **2, 4, 7**, 144 **6**
Société Nationale des Chemins de Fer Français 50 **4, 6**, 53 **1**, 69 **4, 7**, 70 **6**, 91 **2, 4**, 113 **2, 3**, 120 **3**, 123 **7**, 127 **6—7**, 146 **1—2**, 148 **3**
S.C.R. 46 **4**, 124 **1**
South African Railways 39 **2**, 46 **2**, 89 **11**, 91 **4, 6**
Southern Pacific Co., 36 **4**
Southern Railway 148 **4**
Standard Oil Co 36 **4**
Statens Järnvägar 12 **32**
Swedish Travel Bureau 30 **2**
Swiss Railways 120, **5**
Swiss Tourist Office 82 **7**, 92 **6**
Teito Rapid Transit Authority 142 **4**
Toronto Transit Commission 142 **5**
Transportes de Buenos Aires 140 **4**
Union Pacific Railroad 36 **1—3**, 40 **1—2**, 43 **1**, 107 **1**, 113 **1**, 119 **4—5**, 124 **8**
United Press 114 **1**
Viewpoint Project (Norman Tozer) 6, 7, 8, 65 **5**, 56 **2—3**, 58 **1**, 74 **5**, 84 **5**, 84 **9**, 103 **5**, 108—9, 133 **2**, 135 **3, 5, 7—8, 10—11**, 136 **1—2**
Alex Wilson *jacket*